.005

transformations

LIGHT

transformations

LIGHT

Carl Gardner and Raphael Molony

A RotoVision Book
Published and distributed by
RotoVision SA
Rue du Bugnon 7
CH-1299
Crans-Près-Céligny
Switzerland

RotoVision SA
Sales & Production Office
Sheridan House
112/116A Western Road
Hove
East Sussex BN3 1DD
UK

T +44 (0)1273 727 268
F +44 (0)1273 727 269
E-mail sales@rotovision.com
www.rotovision.com

10 9 8 7 6 5 4 3 2 1

ISBN 2-88046-439-0

Book design by Alistair Hall

Production and separation by ProVision Pte. Ltd., Singapore
T +65 334 7720
F +65 334 7721

7   Preface

8   Introduction

16   New Buildings

42   Heritage and Historic Buildings

62   Squares and Public Spaces

88   Bridges and Towers

118   Industrial Plants and Structures

138   Temporary and Narrative Lighting Schemes

156   Glossary

158   Useful Addresses and Publications

159   Credits and Acknowledgements

160   Index

PREFACE

Antonio Gaudí once commented that he could not see how Charles Rennie Mackintosh, his contemporary and in many ways his rival, could produce great architecture in Glasgow – a city where there was no sunshine. I feel sure however that Gaudí's inspiration from the Mediterranean sunshine was equalled by Mackintosh's own sensibilities about the subtleties of Glasgow stone, and the cold, dark Northern Hemisphere light of north-west Scotland.

Light gives our eyes the power of sight, which is the great pleasure-stimulus and life-enriching experience that artists and architects use as their primary raw material. How light has been used by different architects through the ages has always been a great fascination to me – from the Egyptians in their hot sunlight but massive, cool and dark hyperstyle halls to Norway and Sweden's intensely coloured, timber Arctic Circle buildings, built for a climate with limited sunlight.

Of course since the invention of electricity, the last two hundred years have seen an extraordinary and revolutionary extension of what light can do, and the power of the Sun is now harnessed through technology to continue an artificial daylight through the hours of night-time darkness. Growing up as I did in the north of England I am well-used to northern latitudes; having winter days when artificial light is more normal than sunshine. It is no accident of history that the world's first house with electricity was at Cragside in Northumberland, and Blackpool in Lancashire claims to be the world's first town to have street lighting. My parents lived for a while in Blackpool, where the magic of the illuminations transformed what is not the most prepossessing town in daylight, to the most magical world at night that extends the summer holiday festivity season well into the winter.

We now live in extraordinary times, in that the technology of lighting through the use of various media, including film, fibre optics, large screens, and the application of theatrical techniques to buildings, has given the architecture of artificial light almost greater possibilities than that of sunshine and daylight. It is indeed becoming a veritable man-made world at night-time both internally and externally. Not only are existing buildings capable of being transformed well beyond their daytime appearance, but a complete architecture of light is now being explored by architects, designers, artists and sculptors, on a scale which is so large and has such imagination.

It could even be said that the architecture of the future will be transformed through virtual reality techniques, creating distinct possibilities for computer controlled interaction between viewer, artefact and space. Boundaries have become blurred between our real and virtual world as the genius of mankind continues to create his own world within the natural order of daytime and night-time, created by our journeys around the Sun.

INTRODUCTION

Light is one of the most universal and all-pervasive elements in our world. In the form of the Sun, it is the well-spring of all life and drives all our known biological processes, starting with photosynthesis in plants. But it is also the principal 'maker' of the world in another sense, in that it is the medium by which we directly experience our surroundings – without it we would be completely unable to comprehend and appreciate colour, depth, space or volume. Even more fundamentally too, light can determine our deepest emotions and moods – just think of the contrasting feelings elicited by a grey, overcast sky and a bright, sunlit day.

In pre-modern times the absence of light and the hours of darkness elicited fear and were directly associated with supernatural and evil forces – so people generally avoided straying out of their homes during night-time hours. At another level, too, they understood that the presence of light, in its natural form, had the power to transform their lives – witness the wide range of celebratory ceremonies in many cultures around the world associated with the rising of the Sun or the lengthening days of spring.

Yet despite its essential nature and universal presence, light is also one of life's greatest mysteries. This too has long been recognised in many of the world's cultures, such as the ancient Egyptians, who believed that light emanated from the eye of God – or the Druids and other Celtic religions, who put great store in the alignment of the Sun at particular times of the year. For the Romans, natural light had other less mystical but equally fundamental associations with the civic and built environment, and its definition and enhancement. In the Pantheon in Rome, for example, the changing, moving light pattern of the Sun's rays streaming in through the central oculus creates the most important experience of the building.

Newgrange Chamber in Ireland (left) and Stonehenge in England (right) – prehistoric sites where the alignment of the Sun at the winter and summer solstices respectively played a crucial role in religious ritual.

In the work of contemporary lighting artist James Turrell, special viewing chambers are used to 'frame' and represent the sky in its infinite moods and states.

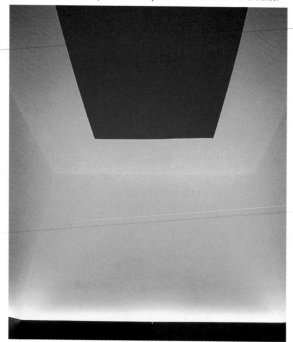 

Artists through the ages too have been inspired and captivated by light, both natural and artificial – and have attempted to capture its mysterious, quixotic nature in their work. One thinks in particular of Caravaggio, Vermeer and Monet, for whom the portrayal of light and its effects on the world around them was an almost sacred task. More recently, contemporary 'lighting artists' such as James Turrell and Dan Flavin have made the manipulation of real light in three dimensions – and the exploration of its infinite dimensions – the object of their life's work.

Even in our own rational, secular age, light retains its mystery for all but the most advanced scientific minds – even Einstein himself was puzzled by the phenomenon. What exactly is light – a wave or a particle or both? And where does colour come from? These are questions whose answers are still complex and provisional, and they will elicit curiosity and wonder for a long time to come.

The Dutch artist Vermeer is one of the foremost exponents in capturing the unique and mysterious effect of natural daylight as it filters through into his finely detailed interiors, ('Young Woman with a Water Jug', c.1662 by Jan Vermeer, 1632–75).

some advances

However, while light retains a degree of mystery, compared with pre-industrial cultures our own society has made considerable strides in the creation and control of artificial light on a large scale. It is extraordinary to think that up until the mid-19th century there had been no significant advances in artificial lighting for around 2,000 years or more – the tallow candle, the oil lamp and the torch covered in pitch or tar are ancient and very limited technologies. Except for the very wealthy on special occasions, they could not be used on a large scale to transform night into day or create vision and spectacle in our urban centres.

The effects of these lighting systems were primarily local – personal tools for lighting the immediate area around a night-time traveller, for example. Alternatively they were domestic items, for illuminating the living rooms in homes – until very recently, people generally retreated behind doors after dark, even in heavily populated cities. While in the 17th and 18th centuries darkness had ceased to constitute a supernatural threat, however, it did become associated with crime and other forms of lawless behaviour – and the main means of combating darkness were still puny and ineffective.

In the early-19th century, gas lighting offered the first form of mass public lighting on a significant scale. But it was the arrival of electric lighting that really freed the general public from the tyranny of darkness. In the 120 years since Swan and Edison developed the first practical electric, incandescent lamps, we have seen the introduction of numerous types of artificial light sources powered by electricity – most notably fluorescent tubes, mercury lamps, low- and high-pressure sodium, metal halide, tungsten halogen, induction lamps, cold cathode and, most recently, light-emitting diodes (LEDs). All these technologies are now at the full disposal of today's lighting designers, architects and engineers and allow them to transform and re-interpret the exterior environment after dark in a way that would have seemed pure fantasy to the Georgians or even the Victorians.

The invention of the first incandescent electric light bulbs by Swan and Edison in around 1880 hugely expanded the possibility of transforming the interior and exterior environment using artificial light.

The V&A's Pirelli Gardens (left) and the Grand Arcade, Regent Street, where lighting designers LDP Ltd. and Pinniger & Partners used carefully controlled lighting to utterly reverse the building's daytime appearance.

These day and night views of the Langham Hilton in London demonstrate clearly how a carefully designed lighting scheme, again by LDP Ltd., can give a new depth and dimension to any façade.

major techniques

Today it is difficult for us to fully appreciate the power of artificial lighting to transform the environment, so accustomed have we become to well-lit roads, floodlit buildings and illuminated monuments. It is worth recapping on some of the key features of artificial lighting that offer us this transformative power:

direction

Natural lighting, from the sky or Sun, comes predominantly from above and has accustomed us to a certain natural pattern of light and shadow. So applying upward beams of light onto a building or structure has a very visually subversive effect and can reverse many of our normal expectations. Features that were traditionally lost in daylight can suddenly be revealed anew. Cornices and window reveals, for example, suddenly appear well-illuminated from below with shadows above them. This reversal of architectural tradition has made some purist architects very suspicious of lighting design.

brightness

One of the most important transformative features of artificial lighting is its (relative) brightness or intensity. Natural lighting is totally unselective in its favours – an overcast sky gives everything a flat, uniform appearance, and even bright sunlight gives vertical and horizontal surfaces a similarly intense blast of light. It's only the relative lightness (reflectiveness) of different surfaces that creates variations in brightness within the environment – for example, limestone will always appear brighter than granite under the same level of daylight.

However, the situation is radically changed with artificial lighting. The lighting designer has the freedom to highlight particular parts of a building or space by applying higher levels of light, which may or may not correspond to its 'natural' daytime appearance – in this way the whole visual hierarchy of the environment can be modified. It is generally true that good lighting design works to enhance and bring out the given architectural form, rather than work against it. Even today, it is not uncommon to hear people say that they much prefer a building's night-time lit appearance to the way it looks by day.

colour / colour rendering

The actual colour of the applied light, and the way in which it renders the original colours of the built fabric itself, are without doubt two of the most important transformative features of artificial lighting. Conventional so-called 'white' light sources vary enormously in the accuracy with which they render the original colours of their objects, and some can hugely distort their appearance. For example, high-pressure sodium lighting tends to have a strong 'orange' or 'gold' tint and very mediocre colour-rendering capability: many types of building material will appear either very 'orange' or their own colours will be completely negated by this type of light.

The key lighting 'tools' of brightness intensity, direction and beam angle are used in combination to give the pencil-like Alter Wehrturm Tower in Germany a most dramatic appearance.

Saturated colour in action: bright red spotlighting of an electricity sub-station in Edinburgh by Jonathan Speirs and Associates, and a green-tinted landscape at Newark Castle.

However, the application of saturated colours, using various types of colour filter, has become a much more common technique in recent years. This offers even more dramatic and controversial transformations of the original subject. In fact, so great is the power of coloured light to create a gaudy, ersatz version of urban reality, à la Disney, that many architectural lighting designers and architects feel that its use should be eschewed except in very specific circumstances. These include temporary celebratory lighting schemes and the lighting of industrial objects or structures with little intrinsic architectural merit. Several examples of this kind of project can be found in these pages.

movement

The most recent innovation in architectural lighting, and one that is still largely at the experimental stage in terms of its long-term potential, is the creation of dynamic lighting effects using both moving light and shifting colours. Computer-operated lighting fixtures with moving beams and rotating dichroic filters – borrowed from the world of theatre and entertainment lighting – are now available on a larger scale for use in exterior lighting. The implications of these technologies for the urban environment are enormous. New, striking lighting effects that were previously the province of artists such as Jean-Michel Jarre can be brought within easy reach of all design and building professionals. As with saturated colour, however, their indiscriminate use could constitute a significant threat to the night-time environment, turning every street and square into a mini-Las Vegas, with all the attendant dangers of light spill, light pollution and glare.

In fact, these threats have already been recognised. Following a number of high-profile cases in the mid-1990s, when logos and commercial images were projected onto the side of historic buildings such as the Houses of Parliament and Liverpool Cathedral, by-laws were passed by some boroughs making such 'guerrilla' actions punishable by fines of up to £50,000.

However, there is one feature of these new technologies that could be highly beneficial in the long run. New computerised lighting systems offer the possibility of interactive, dynamic lighting schemes, which, for the first time, can respond directly to the numbers and activities of their users. For example, colour changes could 'cycle' faster, depending on the number of people present and special lighting 'scenes' can be offered for particular days or seasons (see the Entel Tower case study on pages 104–107).

More prosaically, perhaps, there are already road lighting systems being tested in the UK that dim down to 50 per cent after midnight, when there are fewer cars on the roads. Other possibilities include architectural lighting schemes that 'renew' themselves over time by gradual, programmed changes which present new features of a building and increase their degree of visual surprise.

structure of the book

In this book we have attempted to portray the most advanced uses of these latest cutting-edge techniques and technologies and to demonstrate the enormous transformative power that they have brought to architectural lighting, compared with even 10 or 20 years ago. We have done this mainly through a series of illustrated case studies of recent notable lighting schemes from around the world. For most of these studies we conducted telephone or face-to-face interviews with the lighting practitioners concerned, to tap into their first-hand knowledge of the projects and to elicit their own design intentions. However, we have also added our own perspectives and observations on the merits and successes of these schemes where necessary.

The case studies are grouped into six broad categories, which we believe reflect the main working sites for the best architectural lighting on offer today: New Buildings; Heritage and Historic Buildings; Squares and Public Spaces; Bridges and Towers; Industrial Plants and Structures; and Temporary and Narrative Lighting Schemes. In addition we offer a short Glossary of the major technical lighting terms used in the book to guide the non-specialist reader.

We hope this approach will demonstrate, in the most vivid and engaging way possible, that artificial lighting has a powerful and largely positive role to play in the presentation and transformation of the night-time urban environment in the 21st century, and that the powerful possibilities of lighting as a transformative tool can only increase and develop as the century progresses.

Carl Gardner and Raphael Molony

NEW BUILDINGS

Interest in the potential of artificial lighting and its possibilities has grown enormously among architects, building owners and developers in recent years. As a result, many new structures have integrated exterior lighting schemes from their inception – far preferable to imposing a lighting installation on a building later in its life. When buildings are actually designed with a specific lighting scheme in mind, the results can be truly spectacular.

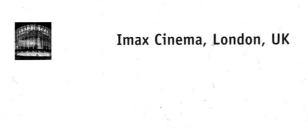

Imax Cinema, London, UK

Estuarine Habitats and Coastal Fisheries Center, Louisiana, USA

Hong Kong Convention Centre, Hong Kong

Efteling Fairground, Tilborg, the Netherlands

Yamaguchi International Trade Centre, Japan

Millennium Dome, London, UK

Miho Museum, Shigaraki, Japan

MAGIC ROUNDABOUT

Imax Cinema
London, UK

Siting the UK's largest Imax cinema in the middle of one of London's busiest traffic roundabouts was a bold move, but it's one that has certainly paid off. For the arresting drum-shaped auditorium has become a fresh landmark in a city that doesn't exactly lack distinctive buildings.

Funded by the Arts Council of England and the British Film Institute (BFI) and built in a mere 18 months, the £22 million circular building was designed by Bryan Avery of UK architectural practice Avery Associates. It houses the 482-seat theatre with its massive 20-metre-high by 24-metre-wide projection screen. The latter, made from perforated vinyl, is used for 70mm presentations in both two and three dimensions.

The 5,000-tonne glass-encased structure rests on a 1.8-metre-thick concrete shelf that is in turn supported by 60 huge damping springs. This arrangement ensures that movie-goers are not disturbed by the rumble of underground trains – only 5 metres below the foundations – that serve nearby Waterloo station.

In keeping with the theatrical nature of the project, the BFI chose a lighting design consultancy with an entertainment background. David Hersey Associates (DHA) is well known for work that ranges from the Treasure Island Hotel in Las Vegas to the West End production of 'Phantom of the Opera'. The practice's expertise lies in translating techniques and equipment from the world of musicals and rock and roll into a vocabulary that works for more permanent architectural projects.

Despite DHA's experience, the exterior of the London Imax presented an interesting challenge. The main auditorium is wrapped in an enormous, specially commissioned artwork by the world-famous painter Howard Hodgkin. This colourful and abstract mural is surrounded by a circular walkway. The entire exterior is then enveloped in a glazed curtain wall, supported by 40 steel columns which rise some 18 metres high.

Peter Fordham of DHA first picked out each column with a narrow-beam pencil of white light from a 150W metal-halide lamp in a Meyer spotlight mounted near the base. The fittings are angled in such a way that each column receives a gentle graze of **white light** while the underside of each cross-arm is also picked out.

Each column and cross-arm is picked out with a narrow-beam pencil of white light provided by a 150W metal-halide lamp mounted near the base.

The main auditorium is wrapped in an enormous, specially-commissioned artwork by Howard Hodgkin, and this is in turn eveloped in a glazed curtain wall supported by 40 steel columns.

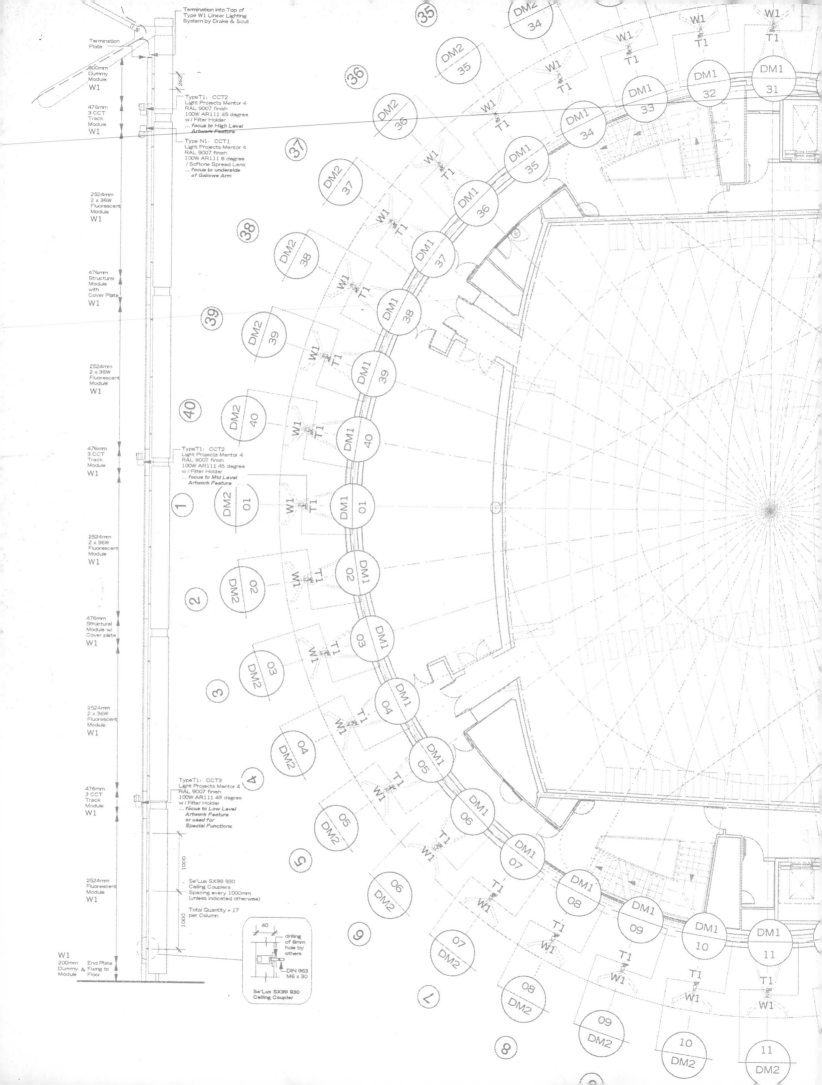

Termination into Top of
Type W1 Linear Lighting
System by Drake & Scull

Termination
Plate

800mm
Dummy
Module
W1

476mm
3 CCT
Track
Module
W1

Type T1: CCT2
Light Projects Mentor 4
RAL 9007 finish
100W AR111 45 degree
w / Filter Holder
... focus to High Level
Artwork Feature

Type N1: CCT1
Light Projects Mentor 4
RAL 9007 finish
100W AR111 8 degree
/ Softone Spread Lens
... focus to underside
of Gallows Arm

2524mm
2 x 36W
Fluorescent
Module
W1

476mm
Structural
Module
with
Cover Plate
W1

2524mm
2 x 36W
Fluorescent
Module
W1

476mm
3 CCT
Track
Module
W1

Type T1: CCT2
Light Projects Mentor 4
RAL 9007 finish
100W AR111 45 degree
w / Filter Holder
... focus to Mid Level
Artwork Feature

2524mm
2 x 36W
Fluorescent
Module
W1

476mm
Structural
Module w/
Cover plate
W1

2524mm
2 x 36W
Fluorescent
Module
W1

476mm
3 CCT
Track
Module
W1

Type T1: CCT3
Light Projects Mentor 4
RAL 9007 finish
100W AR111 45 degree
w / Filter Holder
... focus to Low Level
Artwork Feature
or used for
Special Functions

2524mm
Fluorescent
Module
W1

Se'Lux SX99 930
Ceiling Couplers
Spacing every 1000mm
(unless indicated otherwise)

Total Quantity = 17
per Column

W1
200mm
Dummy &
Module

End Plate
& Fixing to
Floor

40

drilling
of 8mm
hole by
others

DIN 963
M6 x 30

Se'Lux SX99 930
Ceiling Coupler

Eliminating all glare from the scheme for the motorists using the roundabout was a priority (above).
One of many lighting diagrams executed of the exterior wall (left).

In some ways that was the easy part. Lighting London's largest art canvas, at the epicentre of one of the capital's busiest and most dangerous traffic roundabouts, was the real challenge. Eliminating glare to motorists from the scheme was clearly a priority, but the lighting also had to do justice to the artwork. The solution lay in using the inside of the steel supporting columns as luminaire housings. Designed into each of the 40 columns are 10 26W tubular fluorescent tubes, all controlled by digital addressable ballasts. At intervals between the special fluorescent fittings, manufactured by Se'Lux, a short piece of busbar track is used as a mounting for **spotlights** using the fashionable Osram AR111 lamp. These 12V 50W light sources have a diameter of 111mm and a remarkably flat profile, coupled with a very tight beam pattern.

All the lighting is controlled by photocells, and as the evening progresses, the fluorescents dim down while the metal-halide uplights and halogen spotlights strike up.

GLORY ON THE GULF

Estuarine Habitats and Coastal Fisheries Center

Louisiana, USA

Environmental considerations have become increasingly important in lighting design in recent years – the reduction of light pollution and energy consumption being major considerations of contemporary schemes. Unsurprising then that a lighting scheme for a new research and conservation centre in Louisiana, the Estuarine Habitats and Coastal Fisheries Center in Lafayette, kept such criteria well to the fore, alongside strict maintenance and budget constraints. Yet the scheme, designed by Francesca Bettridge and Daniel Rogers of consultants Cline Bettridge Bernstein Lighting, still managed to be 'elegant and seductive', in the words of the International Association of Lighting Designers (IALD) awards judges who gave the project a Citation of Merit in 1999.

The graceful 6,000-square-metre edifice, designed by the architects team of Guidry Beazley and Eskew, rises from the wetlands of the Gulf Coast and includes laboratories, computer rooms, offices and an interpretative gallery, arrayed around its own entrance pool. The aim of the lighting scheme was to enhance the simple, modern lines of the building, while reinforcing the research and marine associations of the site. To this end the lighting highlights the building's various transparent spaces and dramatises its reflection in the waters around it – and also alludes to marine life through the selective use of **blue light**.

The deployment of the interior lighting as an exterior visual feature is a very strong part of the effect. For example, the transparency of the entrance lobby is emphasised by the use of colour-corrected metal-halide **uplights**, which illuminate the wood ceiling, while the floor is lit by PAR38 adjustable fittings concealed within the ceiling panels. The lit image of the lobby is reflected in the entry pool, which is itself defined by low-voltage MR16 lights in the surrounding plinth. Simple PAR20 cans, integrated into the metal pergola, pick out the pathway.

In a similar manner, the view of the office wing from the Interpretation Gallery is accentuated by the use of steplights recessed into a shingled wall. A continuous line of fittings extends from inside the building into the exterior space, to give the illusion that there are no walls between the building and the outdoor area.

At night the colour of the lights creates a **beautiful composition of hues** and sparkling surfaces, all reflecting in the water of the pool and the estuary. The warm sources of the gallery, lobby and offices contrast strikingly with the blue metal-halide downlights in the overhang. The blue reflections in the surface of the sea water, alluding to the marine associations of the building, are further extended by the use of **blue pier lights**.

HARBOUR LIGHTS

Hong Kong Convention Centre

Hong Kong

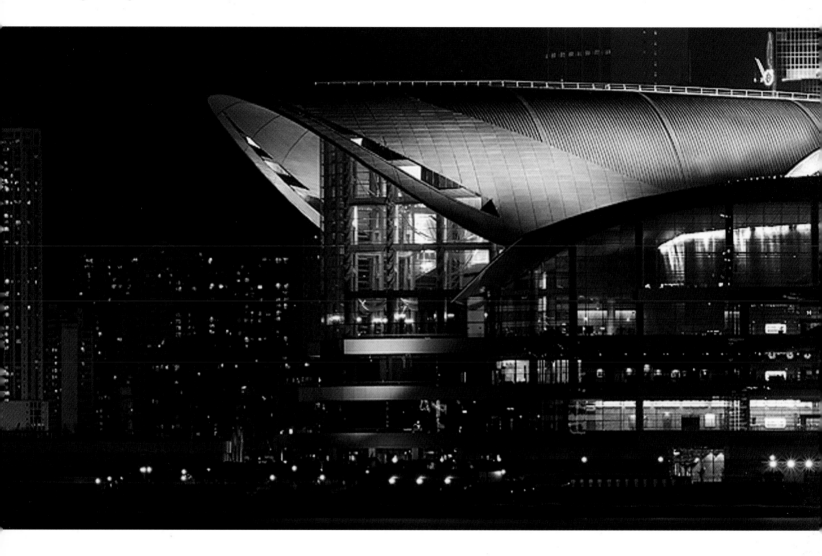

With its awesome setting between mountains and sea, the Hong Kong skyline is one of the most dramatic in the world. The city's skyscrapers jostle for attention and make a very clear statement about the former colony's economic prowess and remarkable resilience. At night, any pretence at subtlety is abandoned and the competition to outshine each other takes on even more urgency, as huge cold-cathode patterns reveal themselves on the façades of otherwise sober offices.

Money talks in Hong Kong, and the transition from former British colony to special administrative region of the People's Republic of China in June 1997 has done little to dent the islanders' obsession with making money – and demonstrating it.

Adding a significant new building to this architectural cacophony, therefore, is not without its problems. Including one that, like the new airport, is designed to bolster confidence before the handover from Britain

to China, is doubly difficult. So when the Hong Kong Trade Council needed a huge extension to its Convention and Exhibition Centre, it knew it was in the market for something dramatic – and yet different from the pack. Two architectural practices shared the brief – local firm Wong and Quyang and the renowned Chicago-based company, Skidmore, Owings and Merrill.

One immediate difference to the surrounding towers of glass and steel was the new extension's location on reclaimed land next to the existing centre. An artificial island measuring 6.5 hectares was created in Victoria Harbour using almost 1,000,000 square metres of sand landfill. And in contrast to the vertical and angular aesthetic of the city, a horizontal, flowing and highly curvaceous concept was designed to house the three main exhibition halls. The halls are stacked on top of each other, and between these and the existing halls on the shoreline is a huge multi-storey atrium with glass walls. All in all, the new building adds an extra 3,800 square metres of space in a part of the world where every square metre is precious.

From the outside, it's the lines of the roof that define the building. They imply movement and flight, and give the impression that the roof is gently lifting off. Clearly, this would be an area of special attention and emphasis for the designated lighting designers, Paul Helms and Christopher Bowsher of PHA Lighting Design of Atlanta, Georgia.

Metal-halide lamps are used to floodlight and articulate the underside of the roof's 'wings'. With a 'cool' colour temperature of 4,000 degrees Kelvin (K), they reinforce the silver and blue of the exterior and crucially add to the floating effect of the roof eaves. The raised roof area is lit with 1kW PAR64 metal-halide lamps with a 'warmer' temperature of 3,000K to provide contrast and amplify its height. An additional row of PAR64s gently grazes the north peak.

'PHA's scheme makes the building appear to glow from within,' said the judges of the IALD annual awards for lighting design excellence, who gave it a well-deserved prize in 1998.

The golden colour of the raised roof area contrasts well with the bluish tinge of the underside of the structure.

PHA lighting wanted to enhance the floating effect of the roof eaves so they decided to articulate the underside of the 'wings'. They achieved this by using halide lamps with a 'cool' colour temperature of 4,000K.

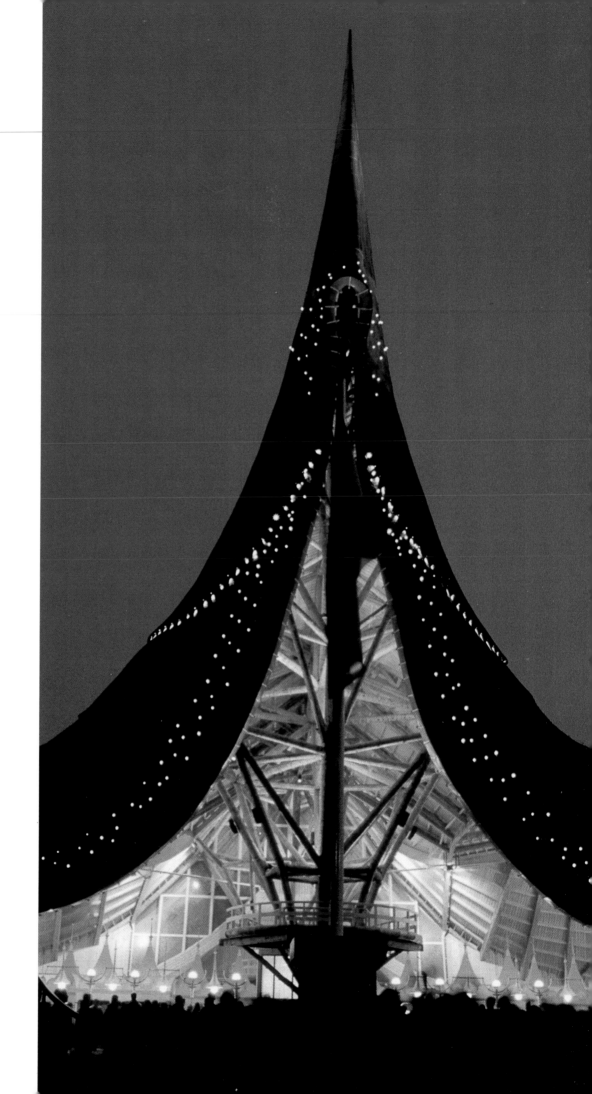

FIBRE FAIRGROUND

Efteling Fairground
Tilborg, the Netherlands

Often restrictions on lighting designers in terms of budget or technical considerations can inspire a more imaginative, and indeed appropriate, solution than if those restrictions had not been there in the first place.

This was the case with Efteling, a peculiarly European fairground of myth and magic in Tilborg, the Netherlands. The extraordinary House of the Five Senses – the theme-park's entrance hall and top attraction – has an entirely timber construction. Over 800 tree trunks support a 4,500-square-metre roof, whose complex curves are covered in straw thatch. It soars from almost ground level to a central peak of exactly 43 metres.

The catastrophic effects of any potential fire forced the designers to opt for a lighting system for the canopy that would minimise the number of heat points, while achieving the light output needed to illuminate the elaborate structure. Maintenance was also a major issue. Replacement of expired lamps with a floodlight-based scheme could be an expensive and hazardous operation. To the credit of the designers, Frans Heijmans and Peter Wiegerinck of Dutch lighting giant Philips, a conventional approach with projectors was eschewed in favour of an effect achieved mainly using fibre-optic lighting.

The beauty of fibre optics is that the light source is remote from the area to be lit and therefore is far easier to maintain. The light output of the lamp is harnessed using special optics and reflectors into a bundle of fibre 'tails', and is piped by internal reflection through the fibres. The output of the fibres themselves is entirely cool – hence its suitability for temperature-sensitive applications, such as in refrigerated units, museum display cases – and straw-covered roofs.

In this case, however, the application of fibre-optic technology was both aesthetic and functional, because the fairylight-like design of the fibre tails, arranged in bands along the roof, was very much in harmony with the architecture.

All in all, some 34 Type 1970 Octopus fibre-optic light generators from Philips were installed. The light source in each is a MSD metal-halide lamp with a rating of 200W. Woven into the thatched roof are 996 optical fibres of both 2mm and 4mm diameter, fitted with conical outlets for **omnidirectional** distribution of light.

However, it became clear that the fibres would not be enough to achieve the full effect, and that additional conventional projectors would be needed to complete the scheme. In particular, the three spires would obviously benefit from clearer definition against the evening sky, so Heijmans and Wiegerinck decided that they should be highlighted, but with a subtle touch. Each spire is illuminated by 400W SON-T high-pressure sodium lamps, housed in NNF 020 floodlights – their colour temperature is a perfect match for the roof lighting.

In 1997, the installation at Efteling won a global Philips Lighting prize for technical excellence. The independent jury praised the originality of the lighting design, which they said was 'admirably in line with the out-of-the-ordinary character of the building, and the meticulous way in which it was realised'.

The three spires were picked out by SON-T high-pressure sodium lamps, whose colour temperature is a perfect match for the roof.

TOWER OF TIME

Yamaguchi International Trade Centre

Japan

The entire upper part of the tower has been turned into a dynamic 'clock' device by lighting the elongated
slots at high level with carefully programmed colour washes, which vary by the hour and day.

Due to their high transparency and reflectivity, modern glazed tower blocks are one of
the most difficult types of building to light effectively. Depending on the angle of incidence of the light,
exterior applied lighting either bounces off the façade or passes through the glass to light the interior.
The Yamaguchi International Trade and Culture Centre, facing onto the Kanmon Straits in Japan, is just
such a building. Almost 150 metres high and covered in glass, it was built as a catalyst and symbol of the
regeneration of a previously run-down city waterfront – and needed a landmark lighting scheme to
attract visitors to the area after dark.

Japan's best-known lighting designer, Motoko Ishii of Motoko Ishii Lighting Design, proved equal to the
challenge by creating a spectacular and unusual lighting scheme that won an Award of Merit in the IALD
awards in 1998. In fact the lighting design fulfilled three objectives: to illuminate the crystalline contours
of the tower; to plot points of light on the tower's spherical crown; and to turn the entire structure into an
original three-dimensional clock and calendar, using light alone.

The building has three main lighting elements. Firstly, its very transparency is exploited by a series of
high-powered **uplighters** behind the glass, which pick out the interior structural ribs of the tower. The
striking effect, silver in spring and summer, and golden in autumn and winter, can be seen through the
tower's glass walls.

Secondly, the spherical dome that crowns the tower is studded with a matrix of white star-like points of
light, created with long-life, electrodeless induction lamps. These brighten and dim every 15 minutes, to
give the extraordinary impression that the dome is breathing in and out in a rhythmic manner.

However, the most notable feature of the building is the conversion of the upper part of the tower into a
kind of dynamic lighting clock. A series of vertical slits in the structure is washed from the inside with a
changing series of colours according to the hour and day – **red** for Sunday, **white** for Monday, **green** for
Tuesday and so on. Each hour is marked with a 3-minute flash of the next day's colour – and on Fridays
and Saturdays, a preset programme is activated, which shows five colours for 1 minute each throughout
the night. The colour changes are achieved using banks of tungsten-halogen floodlights, fitted with fixed
dichroic filters, which are switched in various combinations to achieve the precise colours that are required.

'The building has become an important landmark for the city,' Ishii claims. 'The lighting has added charm,
instilling a sense of a bright future to the people, as if the tower is sending its light to the world.'

CROWN OF LIGHT

Millennium Dome

London, UK

With a price tag of £800 million, Britain's showpiece construction to celebrate the year 2000, the Millennium Dome, was never going to be far from the headlines. Funded by the UK's National Lottery and designed by leading architect Richard Rogers as the housing for 14 individually themed zones, the building is without question one of the most dramatic additions to London in recent decades.

Built on the site of a derelict gasworks on the south bank of the river Thames, the Dome comes with a list of superlatives. For a start, it's the largest dome in the world, weighing in at twice the size of the SuperDome in Georgia. It is 300 metres in diameter and 50 metres high, with 12 angled masts, each 100 metres high. The interior space is covered by what is the largest roof in the world – all 25 acres of it – made from Teflon-coated fabric, so strong that it could support a jumbo jet.

The exterior surfaces of the massive Millennium Dome itself had two treatments – a base
lighting wash created by 48 fixed-beam floods mounted on the masts, plus a moving
colour-change scheme provided by a total of 120 narrow-beam wash lights.

Clearly, the exterior lighting of this enormous – and enormously high-profile – landmark needed some dramatic and eye-catching lighting that would mirror the Dome's image as a high-technology, yet fun, venue. Lighting designer Patrick Woodruffe's main idea was an automated **colour-change** treatment for the exterior canopy that would add dynamism to the Dome's night-time appearance.

In fact the exterior surfaces have two lighting treatments: a **base lighting** 'wash' created by 48 fixed-beam floods fitted with Osram 400W blue metal-halide lamps, mounted on the masts; and the colour-change scheme itself. The latter is provided by a total of 120 Coemar 1,200W narrow-beam wash lights with computer-controlled colour wheels, enabling varied, highly intense colour effects to be projected onto the outside surface.

84 of the Coemar luminaires are mounted on the masts, with another 36 on top of the 12 service cylinders around the Dome's perimeter. Interestingly, the **moving colour beams** look as if they are visible through the translucent fabric and are coming from inside the Dome. While this gives an impression of the activity and excitement inside, in reality, the fabric has a mere 8 per cent light transmission.

Each mast was also **uplit** with four 250W narrow-beam Sill architectural spotlights mounted just above the ventilators at the Dome's surface, plus an obligatory aircraft warning beacon on every mast, each of which is comprised of 10,000 light-emitting diodes. The Dome's substantial overhangs are also lit from below, this time as part of a scheme devised by lighting design practice, Speirs & Major, who were responsible for the internal, architectural and landscape lighting. Their installation uses three 250W 'cool' metal-halide sources to uplight each overhang.

The 12 cylindrical plant towers also benefit from dedicated schemes, this time using tungsten-halogen fittings fitted with red filters. To add a degree of movement and dynamism, this lighting can be dimmed and switched through a control system so they can 'chase' around the perimeter. This dynamic pattern is repeated further out from the building by rows of bollards, fitted with Thorn helicopter landing lights, which are also programmed to 'chase' around the Dome at varying speeds.

From an aerial perspective, the moving colour beams give an exciting impression of the activity within the Dome.

One of the 12 cylindrical plant towers which encircle the exterior of the Dome. Their red colour comes from the tungsten-halogen fittings fitted with red filters used to light them.

SHRINE TO ART

Miho Museum
Shigaraki, Japan

The Shinji Shumeikai is a Japanese religious sect devoted to the ceaseless pursuit of beauty, both in nature and in art, which the sect avidly collects. The Miho Museum is a 17,400-square-metre building housing this unique collection of ancient Japanese and early Western art – and its design by architect I. M. Pei (of Louvre pyramid fame) echoes the sect's own philosophy. The asymmetric structure, determined by the contours of the site, is mainly buried in a heavily wooded hillside, and its materials are all derived from nature.

However, unlike the sect's private sanctuary, the new museum is a public foundation and, when opened, it anticipated about 70,000 visitors a year, all of whom are ferried to the galleries on small electric cars moving along one of two 250-metre-long access tunnels cut through the hillside. These were created so as not to damage the natural environment with surface-cut pathways. Emerging from the tunnel, visitors are confronted by a 120-metre-long bridge over a precipitous ravine, which leads to the museum's entrance hall.

The lighting design, by Paul Marantz, Alicia Kapheim and Hank Forrest of New York-based consultants, Fisher Marantz Renfro Stone, had to reflect the ethos of the site and create a 'sense of peace and tranquillity that is mindful of the environment,' in Paul Marantz's words. In contrast, the goal of the tunnel lighting was to provide a sense of drama and mystery, while allowing the visitor to feel safe and comfortable. Sconces and a linear light shelf, at head height, provide a visual clue to lead the visitor – yet all the lamps are concealed to avoid glare.

During the day, linear fixtures with '**warm**' fluorescent sources, which offer good **colour rendering**, provide fill light to the centre of the tunnel, balancing the high exterior **brightness** of daylight. At night these fixtures are switched off. As visitors approach the mouth of the tunnel, they see the 'spider's-web' lattice of the bridge, half-suspended, half-cantilevered over the gorge ahead of them. At night this is lit with 'warm' metal-halide burial fixtures uplighting the suspension frames, to create a wonderful sense of transition from one distinct type of pathway to another.

At this point, the museum buildings themselves appear as a low-key series of internally illuminated skylights huddled on the hillside. The museum's modest entrance, which has the look of a small Japanese shrine, is framed by accent lights installed in the rear of the stone lanterns on either side of the steps. A series of **uplights** and **downlights** shining up onto the glazed roof transforms the entire building into a soft, warm lantern. The same low-key, yet highly sympathetic lighting treatment, is carried through into the gallery spaces themselves.

The shrine-like entrance to the museum is approached by steps, framed by the accent lights within stone lanterns on either side, while the soft, warm interior lighting creates an inviting ambience in the background (right). The dramatic view from the bridge over the ravine – its suspension cablesglowing mysteriously above, while in the centre, the brightly lit tunnel entrance can be clearly seen (overleaf).

HERITAGE AND HISTORIC BUILDINGS

Historic buildings and structures present some of the biggest challenges for lighting designers, as the lighting treatment must, in general, both respect and enhance the building's unique fabric and cultural associations. For such projects, the use of dynamic and saturated coloured lighting is usually seen as inappropriate – and a more low-key, subtle approach is preferred (the only exceptions being temporary *son et lumière* installations). Considerable attention is also given to the daytime appearance of the lighting equipment – and the minimisation of damage to the irreplaceable building fabric.

Eiffel Tower, Paris, France

 Trinity Buoy Wharf, London, UK

 Albert Memorial, London, UK

 Temple of Luxor, Egypt

INSPIRING ICON

Eiffel Tower
Paris, France

When Gustave Eiffel's eponymous tower was completed in 1889, it was not as universally popular as it is today. Indeed the writer, Guy de Maupassant, allegedly moved house rather than gaze on what he and a large band of influential artists perceived as a monstrosity. Today, however, the tapering lattice-work tower is an inseparable part of Paris and enduring symbol of the city, spawning a million souvenirs. It is used for everything from high-profile political protests to the backdrop for James Bond movies.

The tower has some expectedly impressive statistics – it weighs in at over 7,000 tonnes and is composed of 15,000 individual pieces of metal, fastened by over 2,000,000 rivets, while its four feet are supported by masonry piers sunk up to 14 metres into the Champ-de-Mars. Remarkably, at 300 metres high the construction remains one of the tallest in the world.

Originally built to celebrate the Paris Exhibition, the tower was granted only 20 years of life. It was its use in radio-telegraphy in 1904 that saved it from the demolition that many architects and members of the public felt it richly deserved.

Of course, the landmark has always been bound up with engineering, technology and of course, lighting. From its inauguration, when it was lit with 25,000 gas globes, it has been the focus of experiments involving the latest light sources of its day. So when, some 100 years later, French lighting designer Pierre Bideau was given his turn to make his mark on the tower, he must have felt the weight of history on his shoulders.

However, he eschewed high-tech gimmickry, preferring instead to use field-proven technologies – in particular that workhorse of public lighting, the high-pressure sodium projector. In the wrong hands of course, this tool is the weapon of choice for uninteresting and often light-polluting schemes, but with Bideau the results are inspiring.

French lighting designer Pierre Bideau used 325 high-pressure sodium projectors clustered in groups of four to seven to produce a golden, glowing effect.

The tapering lattice-work tower is composed of 15,000 individual pieces of metal, fastened by over 2,000,000 rivets (left). The view upwards from inside the tower, showing how the floodlights illuminate the exterior from within (overleaf).

The 352 sodium-based floodlights, clustered in groups of between four and seven fittings, are mounted on the structure itself and illuminate it from the inside, so that the steel lattice is made to 'glow' in a most ethereal and effective manner. At the top of the tower, however, lighting is provided by even older, more basic incandescent lamps. Bideau also designed the interior lighting in a superb scheme using Louis Poulsen luminaires.

'My lighting solution proved to be a catalyst for a new general approach to illuminating monuments and squares in Paris,' claims Bideau. 'These areas no longer need to be exclusively functional. We have to strive to create an atmosphere in which visitors feel comfortable, and one that can even evoke emotions and a sense of reverie.'

'As far as the external lighting of the tower is concerned,' Bideau adds, 'the overall task was to give the tower a prominent position on the night-time Parisian skyline, and emphasise the airiness of its structure and design without dazzling nocturnal visitors.'

It's a philosophy he recommends for all external schemes. 'Today it's not just a question of steeping monuments in light, but, on the contrary, of using closely-spaced lighting, of accentuating the various architectural features and the nature of the edifice, as well as giving it a different look to that which people see by day,' Bideau concludes.

Unusually, Bideau also lit some of the interiors of the visitor areas using classic Louis Poulsen fittings.

STRIKE A LIGHT

Trinity Buoy Wharf
London, UK

Trinity Buoy Wharf, on the eastern edge of London's Isle of Dogs, is a group of former naval stores and sheds, today used for arts festivals and corporate events. Its most notable feature is its 20-metre-high lighthouse tower, the last remaining structure of its type on the river Thames, originally used for training lighthouse keepers. In the mid-19th century the Lighthouse was also the location for Michael Faraday's early experiments in electric light, which led to the first electrically powered lighthouse at Dungeness in Kent.

In 1999 the local power company, London Electricity, took the initiative to illuminate various monuments and historic structures along the river. Lighting design consultancy, Lighting Design Partnership (LDP Ltd.), was asked to design a striking new lighting scheme for the Lighthouse and its flanking walls facing the river, which would add a colourful new landmark to the riverside scene in east London.

The structure lies directly across the river from the Millennium Dome at Greenwich (see pages 34–37) – and also due east of the huge Canary Wharf business complex, with its pyramid-topped tower by architect Cesar Pelli. 'Although the Lighthouse is a listed historic building, it is the site of various arts events and corporate parties, so we wanted something with an element of "fun",' explains LDP Ltd.'s project lighting designer, Carl Gardner. 'We also wanted the lighting to make some reference to the Millennium Dome opposite, so we agreed a degree of colour was essential, although without being too garish.'

There are three main elements to the lighting treatment. The flank wall of the adjoining chain store facing the river is illuminated with six 70W narrow-beam CDM-T burial luminaires by Louis Poulsen, while on the taller lighthouse tower itself, four 150W versions of the same fittings are used. Close offset positions ensure that the texture of the brickwork is interestingly accentuated. The lantern body at the top of the tower, with its diagonal lattice structure, is also uplit from the upper walkway, using eight 70W narrow-beam CDM-T Meyer spotlights, fitted with **blue** dichroic filters.

'We felt that the formal blue and white exterior lighting could be emphasised by contrasting coloured interior lighting through the windows,' Carl Gardner explains. So the interior of the glazed lantern is washed with wide-beam 150W Meyer fittings, fitted with amber dichroic filters – a similar treatment was applied to the lighthouse tower stairwells and the two large 'bull's-eye' windows on the tower's flanking walls. To diffuse the light and to avoid exterior glare, the two circular windows were covered with translucent white roller blinds.

'I am particularly pleased with the way that the "**warm**" interior glow of the lantern mingles and contrasts with the "**cool**" blue exterior lighting on the diagonal mullions,' Gardner adds. The final touch – and one further echo of the lighting treatment of the Millennium Dome opposite – is a **red** compact fluorescent marker-light from We-ef Lighting on the top of the tower.

Close offset uplighting of the 19th-century walls reveals the rich texture of the brick, while the 'bull's-eye' windows are made to glow warmly, due to the use of amber filtered floods inside.

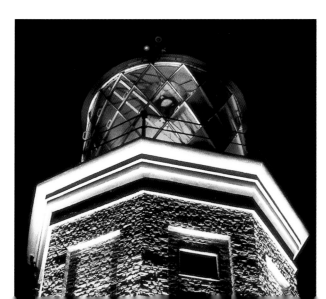

The old lighthouse lantern is given a contrasting colour treatment, with blue filtered metal-halide for the outer drum and lattice, and red floodlighting of the interior.

RADIANT PRINCE

Albert Memorial

London, UK

Viewed from the Albert Hall, one can clearly see the two groups of surrounding statues at each corner and the ornate memorial structure carefully modelled in light and shade.

The famous Albert Memorial in London was commissioned by Queen Victoria after Prince Albert's death in 1859 – but it had deteriorated considerably by the time it was refurbished, at a cost of £11 million, in the late 1990s. Part of the project was a new architecturally sensitive lighting scheme for the memorial by consultants LDP Ltd. that would reveal its principal characteristics – in particular the newly re-gilded figure of Prince Albert himself. So admired was the new lighting scheme that in 2000, it scooped a UK National Lighting Design Award, an IALD Award of Excellence and a UK Civic Trust Award.

The chosen design solution had to rely almost entirely on light fittings mounted at some distance from the monument (only limited attachments to the memorial were permitted). The aim of the scheme was the creation of a carefully controlled hierarchy of **brightness**, with the main focus being the gilded statue of Albert and its canopy above, 'glowing' brightly in the centre of the scene. 'Our strategy was to make Albert, its inner and outer groups of white statues ("the Industries" and "the Continents" respectively), and the crowning crucifix all form two visual "pyramids", one inside the other,' explains LDP Ltd. managing director, Graham Phoenix.

53

Four main clusters of precisely focused spotlights are used for the bulk of the illumination, plus three narrow-beam searchlights at longer range. The clusters of 70W and 150W metal-halide spotlights (28 in all) with various beam angles, colour temperatures and special lenses, were mounted inside four special, architect-designed bronze housings buried in the ground outside the corners of the lower plinth. With a maximum throw of 80 metres, they highlight the outside groups of statues, the white marble frieze at the base of the main part of the monument and the inner groups, with a maximum beam divergence of 20, to avoid light spill across the park.

The frieze in particular is lit using a special ribbed glass lens, to create a narrow, elongated beam shape. 'With all this white statuary, it was very important to ensure that the high luminance of this stonework did not overwhelm the statue of Albert himself,' Phoenix points out.

The gilded statue of Albert, the canopy above him and the crucifix at the top of the monument are illuminated with two other groups of luminaires. Albert is picked out to maximum **brightness**, using two very narrow-beam, 500W xenon floodlights mounted on the roof of the Albert Hall 140 metres to the south – one further fitting of the same type picks out the crucifix and orb. The highly decorative canopy above Albert, which appears to glow from reflected light from the gold statue itself, is in fact lit by four 70W metal-halide spotlights mounted inside the four corner columns (the only equipment actually attached to the structure).

The entire lighting scheme, including the housings, cost around £175,000 – and is controlled by a sophisticated scene-setting control system. This system switches on the various elements over the period of an hour in the afternoon or evening. After midnight, only Albert and the canopy above him remain illuminated, to offer a nocturnal reminder of the ornate, Victorian splendour of this monument restored to its former glory.

A close-up of one of the outer groups of statues ('the Continents') – their white marble finish made it imperative that they were relatively underlit, so they didn't visually overwhelm the main structure.

ANCIENT TREASURE

Temple of Luxor

Egypt

Egypt's historical legacy of extraordinary Pharaonic monuments never ceases to amaze and inspire visitors. The awesome pyramids and splendid temples stand testament to one of the greatest civilisations that the planet has ever known. For the Egyptian authorities, the role of custodian of these wonders of the ancient world is, perhaps, one of its most difficult and sensitive tasks.

So when President Mubarak decided in the early 1990s to rebuild part of the colonnade of the courtyard of Amon Ofis III and illuminate the entire Temple of Luxor, the move was not without controversy. In the end, however, both moves met with the general approval of the experts and the tourists. The project team managed to reconstruct the whole left side of the colonnade, using parts of the original columns that had fallen down, and the night-time illumination followed previous – and relatively popular – transformations at other sites, such as the Pyramids.

Luxor, built on the 4,000-year-old site of the ancient city of Thebes, is one of the most visited places in Egypt – and rightly so. The sheer grandeur of the four temples' architecture has been attracting tourists for centuries. And it was partly with these tourists in mind that the Government wanted to extend the time available for viewing the monuments, while providing a stunning vista for boat passengers cruising down the Nile.

Three main areas were lit: the Path of the Sphinxes; the Luxor Temple itself; and the Courtyard of Amon Ofis III. The main technique chosen was **uplighting**, partly because of the desire not to attach any fittings to the ancient stonework, and partly because the chosen designers, the in-house team at Italian architectural lighting manufacturers, iGuzzini, felt that this technique would emphasise the volume of the architecture.

'We feel that the lighting of the Temple underlines the historical and cultural importance of the age of the Pharaohs,' comments an iGuzzini spokesperson. 'The age was marked, after all, by the monumental nature of the period's architecture.'

However, iGuzzini didn't have it all their own way. The subtle light levels which the company's team planned for the various structures – designed to bring out less-assertive elements of the architecture at night – were significantly increased by the clients, the cultural department of the Egyptian Government, to create a greater degree of spectacle.

The light sources used for uplighting are mainly tungsten-halogen and high-pressure sodium, with 'warm' colour temperatures of between 2,500K and 3,000K, to emphasise the golden tones of the sandstone masonry. The 100W halogen lamps are mainly housed in Woody and Mini-Woody projectors, while the sodium lamps are used in iGuzzini's ground-recessed Light Up fittings.

In some areas, however, such as on the 25-metre-high obelisk erected by Ramses II and the temple façade behind it, 250W metal-halide sources with a much 'cooler' colour temperature of 5,600K were used in Lingotto floodlights, to provide contrast and allow the various elements to remain visually distinct.

The planned light levels – designed to bring out less-assertive elements of the architecture at night – had to be significantly increased at the request of the cultural department of the Egyptian Government.

60

The main technique chosen was uplighting, partly because of a desire not to attach any fittings to the ancient stonework, and partly because the chosen designers felt this technique would emphasise the volume of the architecture.

SQUARES AND PUBLIC SPACES

In modern towns and cities, lighting can play a powerful role in the creation and enhancement of the civic realm – and nowhere more so than in public squares and spaces. In such locations, lighting should be geared primarily to the needs of pedestrians and should help create an atmosphere that makes the users of the space feel safe, secure and comfortable. A successful lighting treatment will usually combine a degree of vertical modelling and illumination of the square's main architectural and landscape features, for visual interest, with more functional elements, such as pathway lighting. In some cases the same lighting can play both these fundamental roles.

Plaza de España, Valladolid, Spain

 Festival Plaza, Ottawa, Canada

 Downtown Helsinki, Finland

 Croydon Town Centre, Surrey, UK

 Peace Gardens, Sheffield, UK

 Smithfield Public Space, Dublin, Republic of Ireland

COOL AND REMOTE

Plaza de España

Valladolid, Spain

The former capital of Spain, Valladolid, is today the administrative and political centre of Castile. One of its main squares, the Plaza de España, was for years the location for the city's lively and colourful fruit market, but the city's planners felt it should be used as a public space – a cool place with water features that would give a little relief from the sometimes stifling heat of the Spanish interior.

The square is based on a central area that covers an underground car park. It has a fountain as centrepiece, and one large area covered by two canopies. These are designed to echo the square's past incarnation, when it was a jumble of market roofs. They also offer an escape from the midday sun.

The lighting of the underside of the canopy at Plaza de España is extremely sophisticated: the metal-halide lamps are mounted remotely, and the light is 'piped' through long side-emitting optical conductors.

The lighting designers, Francisco Alcon Enriques, of Valladolid Municipal Council, and Vladimir Nishnik, of Philips Lighting, allowed for two separate elements: the pedestrian lighting of the periphery and the lighting of the central pedestrian area covered by the canopy.

The latter was fraught with problems and design constraints. Fittings could not be recessed into the ground, which would have been one conventional solution, as occasional markets are still held there. Clearly, the light fittings would have to be integrated into the canopy structures in some way – but maintenance could not be allowed to become a major issue.

The uplighting of the central fountain from the water casts the statue in sharp relief – a dramatic piece of lighting contrasting with the gentle glow of the canopy (left). The uplighting of the fountain on the roadside adds a finishing touch to this elegant square (right).

The solution to this problem was a radical one – remote source lighting. In this type of installation the lamp is housed in a generating 'engine' and the light output is piped, using an optical conductor, like a large fibre-optic lighting system. The difference in this case is that the optical conductor is side-emitting, and its radial light distribution is asymmetric. A graph of its light output around the diameter of the transparent tube shows two pronounced curves where the output is higher.

This arrangement helps put more of the light where it's wanted – on both the underside of the canopy and on the pedestrian area beneath it. In addition, the curve of the roof and the light shade of the wood allow **indirect light** to increase the uniformity of the light across the space.

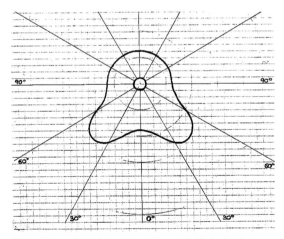

The optical conductor has an asymmetric radial light distribution with two pronounced peaks, one for illuminating the underside of the canopy and the other for the pavement.

66

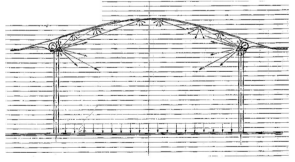

The underside of the canopy acts as a massive reflector that gently diffuses the incident light, adding an indirect component to the direct light of the optical conductor.

The remote source light generators house a 70W ceramic metal-halide lamp. Apart from the fact that this type of source exhibits no colour shift over its life, it was chosen for its good **colour rendering** index of 83, which means that colours appear more true than with alternative light sources.

There is evidence that in warm countries, 'cooler' colour temperature lamps are preferred, whereas in areas such as northern Europe, 'warmer' sources, such as high-pressure sodium, have often been favoured.

The finishing touches for this installation are the uplighting of both the central fountain, which casts the statue in sharp relief, and the fountain along the roadside.

VERTICAL THINKING

Festival Plaza
Ottawa, Canada

Civic squares tend to be lit rather blandly, particularly in parts of Europe, with a high premium on uniformity on the floor – and little attempt to light the all-important vertical surfaces, such as walls, monuments and planting. The re-lighting of the Festival Plaza, Ottawa, by Philip Gabriel of Gabriel Design, broke all these unwritten 'rules' to produce a space that is visually interesting and slightly mysterious, yet comfortable and safe.

Festival Plaza is a large gathering place in front of the regional government building in the centre of Ottawa, with trees, water features and a number of pedestrian pathways. It has to accommodate many special events, such as winter carnivals and music concerts, as well as being a place of rest and relaxation for most of the year. The previous lighting scheme involved blasting the square with orange-tinted, high pressure sodium floodlights mounted on the roofs of surrounding buildings. This created what some lighting designers have dubbed 'the Colditz effect' – flat lighting, harsh shadows and high glare that inevitably has pedestrians scurrying through the space as quickly as possible.

By contrast, Gabriel brought the new, softer lighting treatment right down into the plaza itself. To make it more habitable during Ottawa's long winter nights, he developed a special series of custom-made light fixtures – rows of which are used to 'enclose' the square with a 'wall' of vertical light points, which is balanced and accentuated by the illumination of surrounding façades. The total effect is further enhanced by the addition of small points of **white light** at the top of the row of flagpoles within the square.

The plaza's pools are lit with horizontally aimed underwater fittings, which makes the light reflect off the low, surrounding walls.

These spectacular, custom-made indirect light fittings, using metal-halide PAR lamps, were used to visually enclose the plaza in a 'wall' of light (left). A wider view of the plaza, showing the row of indirect light fittings, fronted by flagpoles topped with additional, twinkling points of light (overleaf).

A view of the masts and uplighter fittings (above).

The plaza pathways were previously lit by high-pressure sodium floodlights mounted on buildings like the one seen here – the soft, low-level, indirect lighting treatment is much more pedestrian-friendly.

The chosen light fittings use an indirect technique, in which the output of the lamp is reflected off a large, white 'sail' or reflector, to create a very soft, diffuse lighting effect in the area around it, with no glare to pedestrians. The luminaire heads, mounted on a curvaceous arm below the reflector, contain 150W metal-halide PAR lamps with a 'warm' colour temperature of 3,000K – the control gear is conveniently located in the base, for ease of maintenance. Unusually, the fittings cost much less to make than conventional post-top fittings, and energy consumption is lower than the old, conventional scheme.

Through the use of a number of perforations in the reflectors, light is also allowed to spill up into the surrounding trees – a device which also gives the top of the reflectors some intrinsic luminosity when seen from behind or above. Elsewhere in the plaza, to add a degree of visual interest, the pools are lit using underwater light fittings aimed horizontally, so the light grazes the water surface and bounces off the low surrounding walls. The **movement** of the water helps to animate this effect.

The overall lighting ambience is calm, friendly and relaxing, with its soft, diffuse areas of 'white' light that makes users appear natural, due to their good **colour rendering** – and the image of the square when seen from a distance is exhilarating and inviting. Yet despite its effectiveness, the solution doesn't measure up to the civic square norm, as Gabriel admits: 'The scheme simply can't be evaluated by conventional illumination measurement, because the plaza would be seen as dark in the middle – yet it still feels safe.'

NORTHERN LIGHTS

Downtown Helsinki

Finland

As an effective way of strategically planning the coordinated night-time appearance of towns and cities, the urban lighting masterplan has become an important feature of the European and US lighting scene in recent years. Denver in the USA, Lyons in France and Edinburgh in the UK are three of the most celebrated examples. However, due to lack of funds or political will, many lighting masterplans have remained unrealised – or have lost their potential impact by being implemented over many years.

All of which makes the masterplan for downtown Helsinki by Ross De Alessi Lighting Design, working with Helsinki Energy's Eero Metso and architect Erkki Rousku, all the more remarkable. The plan, commissioned as part of Helsinki's programme as one of the nine 'European Capitals of Culture 2000', covers the two major Esplanade streets in the downtown area of the city (1.2 kilometres in total) – and was implemented in almost every detail by the city authorities.

Helsinki's streets are illuminated using two versions of the custom-designed lantern in either a single-headed version (left) on the side streets, or the double-headed version for the main thoroughfares (below).

The final *tour de force* of the scheme is the lighting of City Hall using xenon striplights and uplighters to the columns and balcony.

The completed scheme, which won both an IALD Award of Merit 2000 and a GE Lighting Edison Award in 1999, encompasses street, pedestrian and architectural lighting. The major elements of the brief were the reduction of visual clutter, such as poles, trusses and crosswires, the protection of major views and the enhancement of selected historic façades. In addition, the lighting had to provide maximum visual comfort and clarity to the area during the long winter nights experienced in Scandinavia.

Custom poles and contemporary double-headed lanterns with dropped diffuser cones, fitted with GE 35W ceramic metal-halide lamps, were chosen to provide a crisp white light for the road lighting. However, the lanterns, which are both wall- and pole-mounted, were fitted with an additional lighting component on the upper surface, offering the possibility of **uplighting** nearby façades (in the winter) and mature linden trees in summer. This adjustable uplighter component is fitted with a 70W metal-halide lamp controlled by variable-focus optics.

On narrower, pedestrian-only streets adjoining the Esplanades, single-headed luminaires are used. In all cases, the poles, at a lower pedestrian scale than previous lighting schemes, harmonise completely with the architectural styles found in downtown Helsinki – and the **white glow** from the metal-halide lamps better complements the sky at twilight than the previous 250W high-pressure sodium sources.

At City Hall, the plan's detailed design was specially modified to model and articulate its ornate façade with light. Here, miniature xenon striplights with a 20,000-hour life were employed to accent the building's pediment and crest, while low-profile quartz uplights highlight the pilasters on the mayor's balcony and the building corners.

BRAND NEW SKYLINE

Croydon Town Centre

Surrey, UK

With a population of 335,000 and swamped by south London's sprawling suburbs, Croydon is the largest town in Western Europe. But it's also notorious among the UK's architectural and design communities for a different reason – Croydon is a byword for poor planning, ill-considered post-war architecture and general urban blight.

Its copse of relatively tall office buildings – many around 20 storeys – was conceived in the more optimistic period of the 1950s and '60s as showpiece headquarters for blue-chip corporations. However, they now mainly house low-rent, back-office operations of the City of London financial services companies.

The local authority, Croydon Council, has done much to try and alleviate the town's negative atmosphere and image, and has had its successes. In particular, pedestrianisation schemes have been applauded as a counterpoint to the dominance of cars, which speed through the centre on flyovers and underpasses.

 At night, the inhuman scale of Croydon's centre becomes more pronounced and it can take on a threatening, brutal air. Shoppers and office workers evaporate, and the streets are left to young drinkers who frequent the burgeoning number of theme bars.

So when a comprehensive and coherent coloured lighting scheme was proposed for the main buildings in the town centre, it found a more receptive audience than it might have done elsewhere. Indeed, in most other boroughs, the idea of saturated coloured lighting would have been greeted with horror.

The Croydon Skyline Project, as the scheme is called, was developed as far back as 1993 from an idea by Imagination, one of the UK's top design and events companies. Since then the lighting design practice Speirs & Major has been taken on to advise Croydon Council — and the £4 million scheme has won half its funding from Britain's National Lottery, the remainder from building owners and tenants.

Lighting designer Jonathan Speirs organised a number of temporary installations of the colour-change equipment to galvanise support for the radical scheme.

Speirs & Major's Jonathan Speirs proposed a mix of colour-change systems and image projections for the faces of the mainly bland, anonymous office towers – and organised a number of temporary installations to garner support and demonstrate the potential of the technology to possible sponsors.

A 'shoot-out' of suitable colour-change projectors – including Irideon's AR500, Space Cannon's Focus, High End's EC1 and Martin's Mac 600 – was also organised to assess which luminaires were most suitable. In fact, a combination of these different fittings is being installed.

One of the first buildings to be illuminated was, of course, the Council's own 18-storey headquarters, Taberner House. It is lit with 22 Space Cannon 1,200W Focus projectors that give an **ever-changing colour** wash to the front and rear elevations of the building. They are controlled with a DMX system. Slowly, other buildings are being included, the colour-change theme being augmented by strobe flash units and airfield marker lights along the roofs of the buildings.

The scheme is part of a wider strategic lighting plan for the area, which includes improved lighting in high-crime spots, but inevitably attention has focused on the colourful **transformations** of the high-rise buildings. 'It's a fun concept,' says local representative Adrian Dennis, 'but it's got an underlying economic value.'

HEART OF LIGHT

Peace Gardens
Sheffield, UK

Sheffield city centre, in south Yorkshire, has suffered more than most from post-industrial decline, with the virtual death of the surrounding steel industry and the arrival of the giant, out-of-town Meadowhall shopping centre. So the construction of the new Peace Gardens in 1999 was a crucial component of the City Council's 'Heart of the City' regeneration project.

The new gardens, designed by Sheffield-based architects, Design & Property, with lighting design by Equation Lighting Design, were designed 'as a new public focal point in the city centre – an amphitheatre for events such as concerts and public festivals,' according to Equation's director Mark Hensman.

The gardens are situated directly in front of the Grade 1-listed Victorian town hall – and Equation's first task was to light the building itself, 'to create an attractive backdrop for the gardens'. This was done using a series of linear cold-cathode uplighter units, in special troughs, which outline the horizontal features, such as windows and cornices. The circular corner towers are **uplit** with simple metal-halide projectors, to model their shape – and finally to link the upper storeys with the ground, both the rusticated base and first floor of the building are gently washed with metal-halide burial fittings.

The backdrop to the gardens is Sheffield's Victorian town hall, which is delicately lit with a combination of cold-cathode fittings within the window recesses, and metal-halide projectors for the towers.

This view from the back of the gardens shows how the design of the low-level lighting helps to preserve the view of the town hall.

Once the town hall had been made into a central night-time focus for the square, a central requirement was not to obscure it. 'The strategy of low scale and low-level lighting derived from that need – in fact the architects would have been happy if no lighting columns had been used at all,' Hensman admits. In the event, limited use is made of a 5-metre version of the contemporary Se'Lux Quadro amenity fitting, with metal-halide lamps – particularly around the upper, outside area of the gardens. Here too, a number of young trees are fitted with sparkling lines of tiny capsule lamps that vanish into the foliage in summer and reveal themselves in winter.

'The interplay of light and water is a very important feature of the new space,' Hensman continues. At the very centre is a dramatic, multiple-spout fountain – and each of its surging water columns is lit from below by fibre-optic heads, driven by four light boxes buried in the surrounding landscape. The boxes have a rotating colour wheel, so the water can be turned to **red or blue** for special occasions.

Around the square are a number of other formal water features, which bubble up and tumble down from large water bowls, running down towards the central fountain in stone channels on either side of the pedestrian steps and pathways. Here too, lighting was used to animate the display, with underwater fittings mounted in the bowls themselves and at each end of the lower channels. The upper water channels are more brightly lit by recessed tungsten-halogen fittings mounted on either side – an effective, low-level treatment that is also carried through to the pathways and steps alongside.

The ultra-modern water features are well complemented by the sparkling lighting within the cascades and the tree lighting behind.

Cross-lighting the paths and water features from their side walls is far more alluring than conventional, high-glare lighting from columns.

The lighting ensemble is completed by a number of metal-halide burial fittings around the back walls of the outer beds – fittings that will gently **underlight** the plants and shrubs as they grow more mature. Almost everywhere a 'warm' 3,000K version metal-halide lamp was chosen, to pick up the soft, natural tones of the square's buff-coloured stonework.

'The key to the entire lighting treatment was to get people moving into the square and to make it feel comfortable once they are there,' Hensman comments. 'And to do that you shouldn't create the flat, bland, uniform lighting effect that is found in so many urban squares in the UK.'

DUBLIN IN FLAMES

Smithfield Public Space

Dublin, Republic of Ireland

Lighting can play a powerful role in transforming public spaces for new uses. Smithfield in Dublin, in the Irish Republic, is a derelict, former cattle market area, 300 metres long by 45 metres wide. Following the end of livestock sales on the site, it was designated for redevelopment as a new public space for multi-use functions, such as concerts, exhibitions and displays – and with a large international hotel on one side. As part of its ongoing refurbishment, UK consultants LDP Ltd. working with Irish architects McGarry NiEanaigh, were commissioned to design an unusual, highly innovative feature lighting scheme, which would have a major presence both by day and night – and attract people into the space from all over the city.

The solution was a spectacular 'dual fuel' lighting installation with real flare, comprising 12 25-metre-high lighting masts at 15-metre spacings, arranged down one side of Smithfield. Each mast is equipped with a special ceremonial gas burner, supplemented by a large-scale, custom-made indirect lighting system, using curved steel 'sails' as reflectors. This unusual combination produces a striking contrast between the 'warmth' of the gas flames and the 'cool' lighting effect of diffused metal halide.

While the large gas burners at the top of the masts, developed by British Gas, are only ignited for special occasions, the other lighting elements are in use throughout the year. The twin custom-designed uplighter troughs, mounted at around 5 metres on each mast, each contain four 250W narrow-beam 5,000K metal-halide spotlights by Sill Lighting.

'The uplighters can be switched individually to give 25, 50, 75 and 100 per cent of the total lighting output, depending on the time of night and function of the space,' explains LDP Ltd. project designer, Neil Skinner. 'We also chose narrow-beam spotlights so that we could hit the reflectors accurately and avoid light spill and limit light pollution,' Skinner adds.

The reflector 'sails' themselves measure 3 metres by 3 metres and are fabricated in sheet stainless steel with a matt-white powder-coating finish. Two additional 150W metal-halide Lingotto floodlights by iGuzzini are located on the lower corner of each trough, to illuminate the pedestrian pathway behind the masts. On the opposite side, the masts are lit using an indirect lighting technique which is stylistically similar.

The spectacular columns seen by day – the 9-square-metre stainless steel 'sails', painted white, are each lit with four 250W metal-halide floodlights mounted in a trough below.

BRIDGES AND TOWERS

Bridges and towers represent some of the largest, most prominent man-made structures on earth. Often standing alone against a natural background – or separated from their urban surroundings – their strong horizontal or vertical forms offer a very distinctive and imposing 'canvas' for today's lighting designers. In the case of contemporary office towers, however, the use of large expanses of translucent glazing can limit their lighting potential. Often in such cases, designers are restricted to lighting only the crown of the building, while relying on interior lighting to express the building's lower form. Bridges, on the other hand, almost invariably benefit from the proximity of large expanses of reflective water, which enormously increases their lit effect.

Banco Colpatria Tower, Bogotá, Columbia

 Pont de Normandie, Le Havre, France

 Burj Al Arab, Dubai

 Akashi Kaikyo Bridge, Japan

 Entel Tower, Santiago, Chile

 Chain Bridge, Budapest, Hungary

 McArthur Causeway Bridge, Miami, Florida, USA

TOP TO BOTTOM

Banco Colpatria Tower
Bogotá, Columbia

The Banco Colpatria Tower in Bogotá, Columbia is notable for both its height – at 48 storeys it's one of the tallest in the city – and its small footprint, some 30 metres by 30 metres. Beyond that, it is unremarkable in design and architecture terms. Yet it is a testament to both the power of lighting, and the ingenuity of both lighting and equipment designers, that this South American office block has been transformed into a truly exceptional spectacle by night.

Initially, when the bank's CEO, Eduardo Pacheco, approached the talented Miami-based designer, Robert Daniels of Brilliant Lighting Design, the plan was for some dramatic **uplighting** using colour-change equipment. The designers calculated that a scheme based on 300 1kW metal-halide-based luminaires, with additional projectors using powerful xenon sources to graze the tower's corners, would be suitable. Space for eight lighting platforms around the base of the tower was identified, but as the platforms would

The Banco Colpatria Tower is that extremely rare animal in lighting design – a tower that is lit from the top, not the bottom. As it cycles through its various colour combinations, this top-lit effect adds to the drama and intrigue.

have had to jut out onto public space, the City of Bogotá withheld its consent for the scheme. 'After 14 months and four different uplighting designs, we had to try something totally different,' says Daniels. 'Our first thought was to use all xenon luminaires for the uplighting, but Eduardo didn't want the fixtures close to the building entrances.'

At that point, Daniels decided on a new design concept that had never been used in a permanent architectural lighting installation before – lighting the tall building totally from the roof. 'This is a feat impossible for metal halide,' reflects Daniels. 'The only way to downlight the building at that time was to use a horizontal xenon beam, striking an angled mirror and bouncing the light down the wall.'

The xenon-based Space Cannon projectors had to be re-engineered by the manufacturer so that they could be mounted as downlights.

The colour-changing xenon projectors, from the US firm Space Cannon, are designed to operate either upwards or horizontally, so that the correct lamp-burning positions are observed. The first demonstration in December 1997 was only a limited success, however, as the mirror holder frame, built by the architect, couldn't provide a stable reflective surface for the beam.

This is when Bruno Baiardi, president of Space Cannon, become involved. He went back to the drawing board and, by changing the air-cooling patterns of the projector, developed a version suitable for **downlighting**. Its site test, in February 1998, proved that this revolutionary concept was possible.

'Some people believe that it was the fixtures that made this design work,' says designer Daniels. 'Yet in truth it was the combination of the vertical architectural design and the texturing of the jagged, precast concrete tiles that made the lighting succeed. A smooth surface would only cause the light to bounce off and hit the ground, with little being seen from a distance,' he explains. 'Also, by having glass windows that separate the columns, the downlighter beams remain separated, so the individual colouring does not bleed together. This mating of the perfect fixture with the perfect design has resulted in the most advanced building lighting in the world,' Daniels concludes.

STRING OF PEARLS

Pont de Normandie

Le Havre, France

The Pont de Normandie, across the mouth of the river Seine at Le Havre in northern France, designed by architect Charles Lavigne, is the world's longest cable-supported bridge at 2,141 metres – the same length as the Champs d'Élysées in Paris. Opened in 1995, the bridge links Le Havre with Honfleur and forms a key part of the planned 'route des estuaires' motorway system from Calais to Biarritz, down the western shoreline of France.

The bridge's two elegantly splayed 'wishbone-shaped' support pylons, each 215 metres high, dominate the skyline by day – and independent lighting designer Yann Kersale was commissioned to give the structure an equally impressive presence after dark. Taking the river and nearby sea as his inspiration, Kersale chose a predominantly **blue** theme for the lighting.

There are three main elements to the lighting treatment: the illumination of the towers and cable-stays; dynamic lighting of the underside of the roadway deck; and the road lighting itself, which is carefully designed to be an integral part of the scheme. This is in distinct contrast to some bridge-lighting projects where the road lighting, insensitively added by the road-lighting engineers, conflicts with the architectural lighting treatment.

The elegant 'wishbone-shape' support towers are illuminated from below using 96 1kW metal-halide projectors – the outsides of the towers are rendered white, while colour filters make the inside faces deep blue.

This long view of the bridge shows how the specially commissioned road-lighting fittings, all inclined inwards and equipped with added blue marker lights, gracefully supplement the curvaceous form of the structure.

The decorative illumination of the two bridge towers is achieved with a total of 96 1kW metal-halide projectors, most of them located at the base of the towers. Two-thirds of these fittings are equipped with blue filters. While the outside faces of the towers are washed with **white light**, the inside faces of the 'wishbone' structures are picked out in deep blue. Additional projectors are mounted on the bridge deck to **uplight** the inside of the towers above road level.

The second element of the scheme is a series of blue flashing bulkhead marker lights. These are mounted in two lines on the outside edges of the roadway deck's underside, and outline its graceful curve as it stretches across the estuary. An interactive device links their flashing with the density of traffic on the bridge, so at peak times they flash more rapidly.

Finally, there is the exceptional, finely detailed lighting of the road itself – a lighting scheme that certainly transcends the more functional treatment normally seen in such locations. Kersale designed a special road lantern for the bridge in the shape of an inverted boat hull – a total of 480 were manufactured by Thorn. Each fitting has two lighting components – a conventional 250W or 400W high-pressure sodium road-lighting reflector system, and an 18W blue compact fluorescent at the back of the lantern, which adds a small, decorative point of light and echoes the main lighting theme.

The mounting arrangements for the road fittings are carefully designed – horizontal columns would have interfered with the symmetry of the sloping bridge cables, so the columns are inclined at the same angle. Each column is topped by a long, tapering grey spike to prolong the line of inclination. Finally, within the road area bounded by the cable-stays, 84 of the fittings are actually bracket-mounted on the cables themselves, to reduce still further the visual interference with the elegant simplicity of this jewel amongst bridges.

ARABIAN FANTASY

Burj Al Arab

Dubai

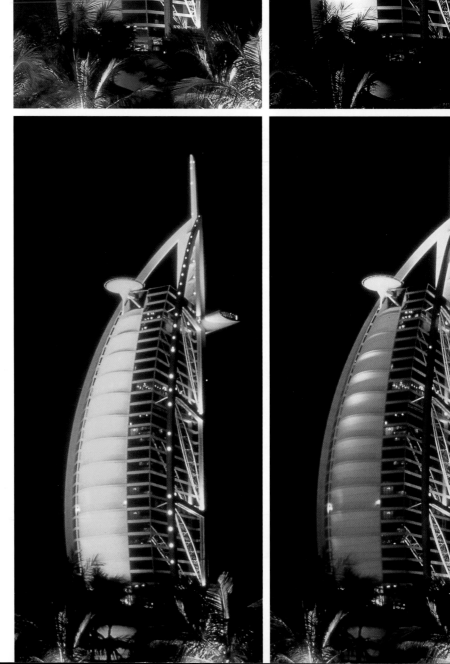

Currently the tallest hotel tower in the world, the 321-metre-high Burj Al Arab (or Arabian Tower) in Dubai is a striking example of contemporary architecture. Its billowing, sail-shaped design – designed to evoke the Gulf's maritime heritage – is a breathtaking showpiece for HRH Sheikh Mohammed's Jumeirah Beach Resort Development.

Rarely has the night-time illumination had so much to live up to. For the appointed lighting design consultants, Scotland-based Jonathan Speirs and Associates (JSA), it was important to do the structure justice with a scheme that both transformed its daytime appearance and yet matched and accentuated its drama. And with a tensioned Teflon fabric wall some 180 metres high by 45 metres wide, they had the perfect canvas. This was clearly a job which called for some of the most innovative equipment in the lighting designer's tool box.

The backbone of the scheme is the Irideon AR500 computerised colour-change projector. In all, some 148 units are used. 58 are on the roof, and are variously focused on the cantilevered 'sky-view' restaurant, the underside of the helicopter pad and the top elements of the exoskeleton frame.

60 more AR500 units illuminate the upper half of the massive fabric façade. These are concealed in planter boxes on the bridge which connects the mainland to the island on which the hotel stands. A further 20 on the island itself light up the lower half. Some of these also supplement the lighting on the helicopter pad, some 200 metres above ground.

The fabric façade also doubles as a screen for massive slide shows and image projections. A number of 10-minute slide shows have been produced for the location, including one on the development of aviation in the Gulf and one on the history of Dubai. Inshore, and concealed in a specially built projection room, are four powerful 7kW PIGI large-format scrolling projectors, aimed at the fabric. At 300 metres, this is the longest throw distance ever for this type of equipment in a permanent installation. The effect is achieved by 'stacking' three separate projected images to make a larger image, 120 metres high by 40 metres wide. The fourth projector is on permanent standby and contains images of politicians and other dignitaries, including Sheikh Mohammed himself, and is used to add a VIP touch when those dignitaries are visiting the hotel.

Flashing units, called strobes, have also been installed along the sides of the exoskeleton running right up to the top of the spire. The units, 90 High End Systems Dataflash luminaires, are individually addressed by the control system and can flash randomly or have pre-programmed sequences such as chases and patterns.

The crowning glory on this tower is four 7kW Skytracker searchlights that sweep the sky with **moving pencil-beams of light**. The control system for the project was designed in conjunction with JSA's New York-based sister company Focus Lighting and is designed to ration the effects, so that the lighting doesn't become excessive. 'The lighting shows are designed so that the effect is not too kinetic,' says Speirs. 'We want it to be colourful, hypnotic, fun and expressive.'

A view of the tower in the daytime. At an amazing 321 metres high, the Burj Al Arab is currently the tallest hotel tower in the world, and is truly an original and inspiring modern construction.

SHINING SPAN

Akashi Kaikyo Bridge

Japan

Nearly 4 kilometres long in total, with a central span of 1,991 metres and twin support towers 300 metres high – the height of the Eiffel Tower – the Akashi Kaikyo Bridge is the longest suspension bridge in the world. Opened in 1998 to cross the Akashi strait between Honshu and Awaji islands, the bridge has been constructed to withstand an 8.5 Richter magnitude earthquake with its epicentre 150 kilometres away.

Such a record-breaking bridge demanded decorative lighting that would reflect this supremacy – but concurrently, the size of the bridge makes the maintenance issues enormous. Regular re-lamping would be a logistical nightmare, and as the bridge crosses a busy shipping lane, illuminance at water level had to be low, to avoid disturbing the visual field of navigators.

'We wanted to create a graceful night-time landmark, whilst at the same time enhancing the bridge's structure,' explains the award-winning lighting designer, Japan's own Motoko Ishii. 'The lighting had to be free from disturbance to both road traffic and shipping… and all with the minimum expenditure of electrical energy.'

A daunting lighting design project – the Akashi Kaikyo Bridge in Japan, at 4 kilometres in length, with a central span of almost 2 kilometres, is the longest suspension bridge in the world.

The lighting begins by accentuating the vertical. The green-grey towers and the closest vertical cable-stays are conventionally illuminated in white, with well-louvred metal-halide floodlights located at the base of the tower, to shield them from view. Then the decision was taken to outline the sweep of the main support cables, using clusters of 27W **high-brightness** induction lamps.

This relatively new technology offers an electrodeless lamp with a life of around 80,000 hours – enough for 20 years burning, from dusk until 11pm each day, before replacement. The new lighting scheme can withstand wind speeds of 80 metres per second, and the energy bill is very small. Although there are 3,250 lamps involved, the running cost is only in the region of £4 per hour.

The bridge's main support cables are outlined using a total of 1,084 special induction lamps, with a red, blue and green component, so the colour effect can be varied for different seasons and times of year.

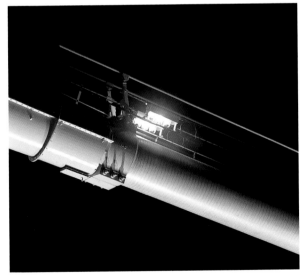

Close-up of the induction luminaire housings on the upper surface of the main support cable, which can offer combinations of up to 28 colours – including a rainbow pattern on the hour, every hour.

Each of the 1,084 clusters that outline the support cables incorporates a **red**, **green** and **blue** lamp. These can be switched in combination, using a computer-controlled programme to achieve a range of 28 colours, including various **pearly hues** (pink, yellow and so on). These are activated for different seasons, or to celebrate special events. For example, the bridge appears red and white at New Year, green in spring and blue for the summer holidays. And on the memorial day for the Great Hanshin Earthquake of 1995, the bridge is lit in pearl white, with no colour changes, and the lighting dimmed to 50 per cent. The bridge also acts as a form of clock – on the hour, every hour, for 5 minutes a rainbow pattern lights up the sky.

SANTIAGO SPECTACLE

Entel Tower
Santiago, Chile

The illumination of the Entel Tower in Santiago, Chile, back in 1994 has become iconic among lighting designers and architects. The 128-metre-high communications tower of Entel Chile – the country's largest telecom company – was the first major structure in the world to have an automatic colour-change lighting treatment. Up until then, buildings lit with colour, such as New York's Empire State Building, used filters that were manually changed every day.

The daring project had a certain inevitability for three reasons. Firstly, Entel, previously the state-operated telephone company, was looking for an innovative way of marketing itself effectively against a host of new private companies. Secondly, Focus's principal Paul Gregory knew a lot about colour – he had lit 'Saturday Night Fever' in the 1970s and, following the movie's huge success, had been commissioned by many of the

The changing night-time appearance of the Entel Tower. The 128-metre-high tower became, in 1994, the first major structure in the world to have automatic colour changing.

major nightclubs around the world. Finally, in the early 1990s, US entertainment lighting manufacturers VariLite developed a version of its rock and roll colour-change projectors for exterior, architectural applications – and was keen to try them out in a major public project.

The VariLite unit, the AR500, uses a patented arrangement of computer-controlled dichroic filters and can produce a full spectrum of saturated hues, which can be changed instantly in infinite combinations. Along with associate designer Douglas Cox, a former theatrical lighting specialist, and lighting artists Alejandro and Moira Sina, Gregory devised a dramatic AR500 scheme that would transform the night-time appearance of this brutal, concrete landmark tower and make it visible from the Andes.

One of the banks of 20 AR500 units which lights up one face of the four-sided tower. This bank is located on the roof of an adjacent building.

A total of 80 AR500s with 700W metal-halide light sources were installed in four banks of 20 units, each aimed at a different face of the tower. The banks were located on the roofs of adjacent buildings, except for one mounted on two 10-metre steel poles across the street. The final *coup de grâce* was provided by six motorised searchlights mounted at the top of the tower. Programmed by Douglas Cox, the Xenotech Brightlight units are fitted with powerful 7kW xenon lamps and angled at either 90 or 45 degrees from the horizontal. Additionally, they can all combine to point straight up into a 1-mile-long beam.

'The possibilities are endless,' says Paul Gregory. Custom software allows huge flexibility in programming the projectors and, apart from a nightly sequence of colour changes, special occasions such as New Year's Eve can be marked appropriately. 'The sky is darker in Santiago, so the colours really shine,' Cox adds. 'The effect is like a fantastic pillar of light. And even if you can't see the tower, you can see the beams shooting up into the night sky.'

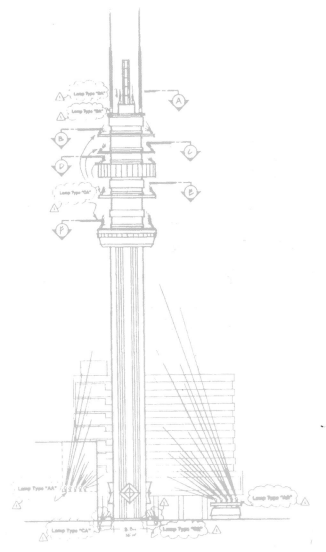

This diagram shows the location of the six motorised searchlights at the top of the tower, and also the angle of light from the AR500 units below.

The six motorised searchlights mounted at the top of the tower are fitted with a powerful 7kW xenon lamp and are either angled at 90 or 45 degrees, or combine to point straight up into a 1-mile-long beam.

SPARKLING GIFT

Chain Bridge

Budapest, Hungary

Designed by British engineer William Tierney Clark in 1840, the Chain Bridge is an enduring symbol of Budapest. Linking the two parts of the capital, Buda, which sits high on the western bank of the Danube, and Pest, which extends from the eastern side, the elegant suspension bridge is one of seven crossings of the Danube in the city. It is one of only two Tierney Clark-designed bridges that survive – the other is the similar, but smaller, Marlow Bridge across the Thames in England.

The Budapest bridge is known as the Széchenyi Chain Bridge and is named after Count István Széchenyi who, in 1839, appointed Tierney Clark as architect of what was the first permanent bridge across the Danube below Vienna since Roman times. Sadly it was destroyed in World War II, but it has since been faithfully reconstructed.

To mark the 150th anniversary of the construction, GE Lighting – the General Electric division with extensive lamp-manufacturing facilities in Hungary – offered to light it as a gift to the people of Budapest. Although the bridge had been lit before, the new scheme would represent a radical transformation due to the availability of new lamp technology.

Metal-halide discharge lamps with conventional quartz arc tubes have many qualities, including high output, good energy efficiency and far better **colour rendering** than most other discharge lamps. But they have one drawback, which could have been cruelly exposed over the 330-metre span of the Chain Bridge. Over the life of the lamps, they tend to shift their colour appearance, or colour temperature. Not only that, but each individual lamp ends up with its own unique colour, often shades of **green**, **red** and **blue**. Clearly, an installation with traditional metal-halide light sources on this bridge would soon have deteriorated into an uncontrolled confusion of colour.

the decorative detail of the suspension elements was picked out by around 1,178 low-energy compact fluorescent lamps, manufactured locally in Hungary.

The development of new-generation metal-halide lamps has solved the potential problem of too many confused colours. The lamps use a different gas mixture in the arc tube, which is ceramic rather than quartz, so they can burn hotter. This effectively arrests the colour shift and helps maintain a crisp white appearance throughout their life. GE Lighting had developed its ceramic metal-halide range by 1999 and was keen to find a showpiece for it. The Chain Bridge was the perfect choice.

A total of 260 ceramic lamps are used to floodlight the main structure of the bridge. New luminaires were fitted to the existing supports, and the required effect was achieved by sandblasting the glass faceplates and using custom-designed hoods and shielding plates. They were then painted to blend in with the mounting positions: a limestone colour for those luminaires on the stonework, or dark grey for those on the metalwork.

Some 1,178 low-energy compact fluorescent lamps, also made locally in Hungary, were used to enhance the festoon nature of the suspension elements. Not only is the scheme far more energy-efficient than before – in fact electricity consumption has decreased by 67.5 per cent – but it also represents the best practice in projects of this kind. The emphasis is not on blasting the bridge with light, but more on emphasising its architecture and making it appreciable by a night-time audience.

Designer's sketch of the existing supports (above) to which the luminaires were fitted (below). To achieve the required effect, the glass faceplates were sandblasted and custom-designed hoods and shielding plates were used.

PEOPLE'S CHOICE

McArthur Causeway Bridge

Miami, Florida, USA

Despite its gently flowing road lines and wine-glass supports, the McArthur Causeway Bridge in Miami, Florida is not the stuff of architectural magazine spreads or travel programmes. No Pont de Normandie or Golden Gate, this is a prosaic structure with a job to do. The areas it immediately connects are not the glamorous neighbourhoods of Miami, but quite the reverse. Indeed, the structure's architecture is not even unique – the design comes right out of the US Department of Transportation's civil engineering handbook.

The Port of Miami, who are the owners of the bridge, were never bent on making a design statement – it was only years later, when urban beautification projects became fashionable across the world, that the bridge was noticed by the city fathers. The authorities knew that here was a 'quick win' in terms of urban renewal. Lighting was already proving itself across the world as one of the most high-profile media of

regeneration, and the bare concrete canvas of the bridge was perfect for painting with light.
Not only that, Miami was also home to the award-winning practice, Brilliant Lighting Design, whose principal, Robert Daniels, had won plaudits for his work on the transformation of the Banco Colpatria tower in Bogotá into a night-time spectacle (see pages 90–93).

Clearly, colour was to have an important role to play if the edifice was to have eye-catching appeal, but it couldn't be allowed to affect the motorists on the busy roadway. 'Our design was perhaps unique, in that it is possibly the first bridge lighting in the world to be created with all the following design concepts: energy efficiency; an extra-long maintenance life; anti-vandalism; and, of course, beautification,' Daniels claims.

The backbone of the scheme is provided by some 279 spotlights, mounted both below and on the sides of the bridge to wash the concrete. Each fitting has a wide beam and uses a long-life metal-halide source. Additional glass colour filters are mounted on the front of each fitting. The exact choice of colours was a big issue. Unlike a colour-changing scheme, where the lighting designer is often given creative freedom to select the hues and combinations he or she feels are most appropriate, a permanent colour installation provokes strong opinions. Colours have strong cultural associations, so the local political authorities came down to the bridge to vote on various colour combinations. Surprisingly, magenta was a popular choice.

The metal-halide fixtures were augmented by 334 spotlight fittings, fitted with GE Lighting's mercury vapour lamps, plus 220 simple 48-inch fluorescent tube **striplights**, again with colour filters. Some of the fittings were used by Daniels simply to create reflections on the water. The location of the bridge also merited strong anti-vandalism measures. The fixtures were buried into concrete vaults and fitted with cover grates to prevent theft on the land-side piers.

The installation has proved a big hit with the people of Miami, and in 2000 earned Daniels and his team an Edison Award of Excellence from GE Lighting for installations which use its lamps.

116

The colourful scheme designed by Miami-based lighting designer Robert Daniels is out of view to motorists using the busy crossing.

The design of the McArthur Causeway Bridge is far from unique. It has been taken directly out of the US Department of Transportation's civil engineering handbook.

INDUSTRIAL PLANTS AND STRUCTURES

Factories and industrial facilities can represent extremely attractive projects for exterior lighting treatment. Whether newly constructed or traditional 'rust-belt', they are usually large, complex canvases with interesting shapes, structures and textures. In the main, they are located away from centres of population – and consequently free of the many restrictions inherent in comparable-size buildings in cities. A well-executed scheme, often using coloured and dynamic lighting, can re-awaken interest in what otherwise might be considered obsolete and ugly.

Tyseley Waste Plant, Birmingham, UK

 City of Bridges, Cleveland, Ohio, USA

 Landscheftspark, Duisberg-Nord, Germany

 Cranhill Water Tower, Glasgow, UK

INDUSTRY INTO ART

Tyseley Waste Plant

Birmingham, UK

Unlike other transformations of 'rust-belt' buildings in this book, the owners and architects of the Tyseley Waste Plant on the outskirts of Birmingham, UK, saw light as an integral component of the building from the outset. It was designed into the project's fabric in a way that is, unfortunately, all too rare in contemporary construction.

The transformation of what some might regard as an industrial eyesore into a vibrant, innovative work of art and highly regarded landmark came about through a unique collaboration between companies, agencies, architects and artist. The City Council in Birmingham – a conurbation which has suffered from

The artist Martin Richman's rendering of the four giant light boxes (overleaf).

Transforming what could be an eyesore into a vibrant and innovative work of art and landmark for Birmingham
was the result of a unique collaboration between companies, agencies, architects and artist (below).

poor post-war planning and some cruelly dated architecture – has a policy of encouraging the private
sector to set aside a percentage of building costs for the commissioning of art.

As enthusiastic supporters of the policy, both Birwelco, the plant's builder, and Tyseley Waste Disposal, the
plant's owner and operator, welcomed the involvement of the Public Art Commission Agency (PACA) in
finding an artist to collaborate on the project. One of Britain's leading lighting artists, Martin Richman,
was chosen to work with the architect, Ray Perry of Faulks Perry Culley & Rech, to create a special
marriage of industrial engineering and art.

Richman picks out the surrounding metalwork through the use of red floodlights.

Richman believes in respecting the integrity of the buildings he works on. 'I am not interested in concealing the structure but revealing it,' he says. 'I don't want to pretend it is anything other than what it is. I try to be as true to the form of the building as I can be.' With Perry, he designed a dynamic lighting installation that would work with the rectilinear lines of the facility. Translucent and transparent cladding was installed in selected areas – including four giant light boxes on the building's most visible façade – to maximise the external impact of the lighting.

Richman then used AR500 colour-change projectors, linked to a Pulsar Masterpiece lighting controller, to turn these translucent light boxes into canvases of **changing light**, visible to motorists on the busy main road nearby. Solid bars of **shifting colour** were

also created by installing 100-mm-wide
polycarbonate light pipes, each up to
12 metres long, driven by 200W metal-
halide sources.

The main plant ducting was illuminated with
400W blue metal-halide floodlights. Finally,
two red floodlights pick out the metalwork
and an Optikinetics K4 gobo projector
illuminates a translucent window with a
changing scene. 'The final outcome is a new
landmark for Birmingham, visually striking
in the daytime and ethereally beautiful at
night,' says Vivien Lovell of the PACA.
'Martin Richman has deftly spun the
potentially mundane into something beyond
the functional aesthetic originally envisaged.
The result is an enlightened interpretation
of public art.'

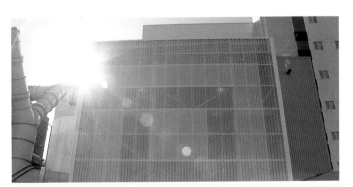

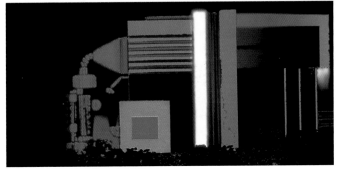

From the outset, the dynamic lighting installation was designed to work
with the rectilinear lines of the facility (above and below).

OVER THE WATER

City of Bridges
Cleveland, Ohio, USA

With a healthy budget of $4.2 million, lighting designers Ross De Alessi and Brian Lockwood lit 18 of the city's 24 river crossings in a scheme that has turned the Cuyahoga river into a fairground of brilliantly lit bridges.

Cleveland, Ohio has experienced the stereotypical stages in the lifetime of an industrial city – rise, decline and renewal. But with Cleveland, it has all been more pronounced – the highs have been higher, and the lows lower than most comparable US urban centres.

The place prospered as a trading centre and railroad hub in the 19th century, reaching its apotheosis in the 1920s, when it was the sixth largest conurbation in the USA. However, in the years following the Great Depression, it went into a long, and seemingly relentless, decline that saw thousands of jobs and people leave the city. The legacy of Cleveland's industrial heritage is most visible along the looping Cuyahoga river. Here hulking steel bridges of a bewildering variety stand as mute witnesses to an age when engineering was omnipotent.

Lighting, too, played a large role in marking Cleveland's successful past. Electric lamps were used on a triumphal arch to mark the city's first 100 years, and the Industrial Exposition of 1927 saw an enormous tower studded with glass crystals lit by 36 searchlights. It was fitting, therefore, that when Cleveland came to celebrate its bicentennial in 1996, it chose these bridges as both a focus for revitalisation and as a medium for a celebration of lighting that won plaudits and recognition around the world.

The lighting designer, Ross De Alessi, of the eponymous Seattle-based practice, worked with his colleague, Brian Lockwood, on a scheme that would turn the night-time vista into a wonderland of lighting. Appropriately, it became known as the 'City of Bridges' project. With a healthy budget of $4.2 million, and a broad design brief, the pair drew up designs for 18 of the city's 24 river crossings. Six were lit for the bicentennial event in a feast of theatrical, **dynamic colour.**

The 250W lamps on either end of the Willow Avenue Bridge are just one instance of this project's bold use of colour.

'The bridges' past, their shape and the way they span the river determined how we approached them... and how we celebrated their history,' says De Alessi. 'Wherever there is a working part of a bridge that's of interest, we highlighted it, so that when people are waiting for it to open, or close, they can enjoy the movement and the celebration of it all.'

Bascule One, a disused rolling lift bridge with a railway at its base, has a dramatic light show every half-hour. Mist pours down from concealed nozzles on the upper steel plates, while rows of uplights – fitted with PAR56 lamps and dichroic filters in a variety of warm colours from red to amber – switch in pulses, to mimic the fire and heat of a steel forge. The inferno effect is maintained for a few moments and then it reverts back to the bridge's 'cooler', standard illumination, using 150W high-pressure sodium lamps. The Willow Avenue Bridge is next to the river's entry, and it remains open for long periods to allow passage for barges laden with ore. The structure's lighter colour allowed lower power fittings to be specified – a mixture of 175W and 250W metal-halide fittings are mounted both on poles and on the main rising span of the bridge, to highlight its colour and texture. At each end of the upper structure, where the huge motors are housed, a dramatic multi-coloured effect is achieved with a row of 250W PAR lamps with coloured filters.

These playful effects are continued in Bascule Two, another inoperative bridge, where the passage of a 'ghost train' is created using lighting. The train's approach is mimicked by the warming up of a 2kW metal-halide floodlight aimed up the raised arm of the bridge. When it attains full output, two 1kW metal-halide PAR64s switch on. When the ghost train 'collides' with the trestle section, a 1kW xenon searchlight strikes, delivering a powerful blast of light.

The Eagle Avenue Bridge, a unique, vertical lift bridge, is the most visible from the city centre. To avoid glare to both motorists and the ships on the Cuyahoga from the fittings which highlight its pulleys and towers, some of the fittings had to be cantilevered off the north side, so that the structure could be illuminated in both its open and closed positions. However, the row of 50W fittings mounted on the undercarriage could still lead to glare to boatmen. This necessitated an extremely clever solution involving photocells. If a ship's pilot wants to kill the lights, he shines a searchlight at the photocells and the row of fittings is extinguished for a few minutes.

BRIGHTENING THE RUST

Landscheftspark
Duisberg-Nord, Germany

The commission to transform a redundant ironworks in Germany using light was something of a departure for British designer Jonathan Park. Park made his name in rock and roll and entertainment lighting, and his credits include the acclaimed 'Voodoo Lounge' tour by the Rolling Stones in the mid-1990s, as well as staging for groups from Pink Floyd to U2.

Park's practice Fisher Park teamed up with Lighting Technology Projects (LTP) to fulfil this unusual and ambitious brief. The project was to illuminate the rusting metallurgical behemoths of the Landscheftspark Duisberg-Nord in north-west Germany. LTP had experience of applying theatrical techniques to buildings, having been involved in two large-scale projects in their home city of London: the blue wash on the Earls Court Exhibition and Concert Hall and the eerie green glow of the Hoover Building, a former vacuum-cleaner factory in west London.

However, the Duisberg job was very different. First of all there was the sheer size of the project – the ironworks is on a 1-mile-square site, and some of the steelwork is over 80 metres tall. Unusually for Park,

BELT

The dramatic scheme which transforms the redundant ironworks – including the 80-metre-tall chimneys – into a nightly light show was created by the British rock and roll specialists Fisher Park.

the project demanded a permanent exterior lighting scheme, while LTP had to create an animated, computer-controlled installation, effectively a *son et lumière* without the *son*.

'What we were trying to achieve was based on two fundamental aspects of monumental and architectural lighting,' says LTP's manager for the project, Bruce Kirk. 'Monumental in terms of lighting very big objects that are spread apart – architectural in terms of how the building was perceived in terms of its structure and the memory of its industrial application, evidenced by the blast furnace and pipework.'

'The lighting scheme was devised to accentuate the structural envelope from all perspectives, whether within the ironworks, in its grounds or on the autobahn several kilometres away,' Kirk continues. 'And we wanted to do it all with an animated, **multicoloured** system of light – the idea being that we could produce a lighting environment that could change on either a nightly or even hourly basis. Intellectually our client found it all very interesting, but practically they weren't sure whether it would work, or whether they agreed with it or not.' Fortunately, they did eventually agree.

Designer Jonathan Park used over 400 projectors, mainly with 250W and 400W metal-halide sources, to light the plant, and connected all of them to a 100-circuit computer.

The lighting scheme is such that the form of the ironworks can be appreciated from every perspective (above and below).

Park's concept is realised using over 400 projectors, mainly with 250W and 400W metal-halide sources, all switched via relays and a 100-circuit computer. A series of different lighting programmes was devised for the various events planned at the venue, which houses a semi-open-air auditorium in one of the metal casings.

The lamps were mostly self-coloured **blue** and **green**, but these are combined with hard-glass filters in mainly **red** and **yellow**, to provide more saturated hues. 60 small bulkheads with 9W compact fluorescent lamps punctuate the scheme, creating dotted lines up the three enormous chimneys. Each chimney is also illuminated by six metal-halide floodlights – two at each of the three sides. Mounted some 50 metres away, they're tightly focused on the features using a special lens system.

The final dramatic touch is provided by 72 pieces of cold-cathode tubing that create a halo effect around the top of the rusting structures.

TOWER OF POWER

Cranhill Water Tower

Glasgow, UK

Cranhill, on the eastern fringes of Glasgow, is an estate of predominantly run-down council blocks, with a significant unemployment and drug abuse problem. This socio-economic background is what makes this project even more admirable and unusual. This was a community-driven project to make its local watertower into a prominent landmark on the main M8 motorway into the city, using a distinctive lighting treatment. The scheme's merits were recognised in 2000 through the winning of the Glasgow Institute of Architects' Award and a Distinction in the UK's National Lighting Design Awards.

The tower, one of nine similar structures dotted around Glasgow, was built in the 1950s and is more than 25 metres high. In 1997 the local community group came up with the idea to make the tower and its surrounding land into a sustainable public space, with a new garden and permanent lighting installation. Chris Stewart Architects worked with the group over the space of two years to turn this concept into reality. 'As part of a larger masterplan to potentially light all these towers, each one was given the name of a planet in the solar system,' comments Adrian Stewart, from Chris Stewart Architects. 'As all the streets in Cranhill are named after UK lighthouses, Neptune was the obvious choice for this one.'

Following a series of test lighting demonstrations in 1998, the permanent scheme was installed in late 1999 with the help of Northern Lights, who realised the installation, and Philips Lighting, who supplied the equipment. The project immediately attracted considerable media attention. 'The main idea was to "float" the heavy concrete structure on a bed of light which would be visible for miles around,' Stewart explains. This was to be achieved by first washing the central soffit of the tower in **green-blue light** from below, so its reflected light bounces off the inside of the perimeter columns.

The lighting design strategy is to 'float' the main structure on a bed of light – this is created in part by washing the inside soffit of the tower with green-blue light from filtered metal-halide spots around the base.

Standing by one of Glasgow's busiest motorways, the Cranhill Water Tower is one of nine such structures in the area – and the first one to be subject to a decorative lighting scheme devised by the local community.

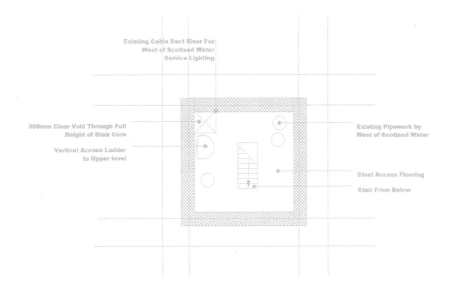

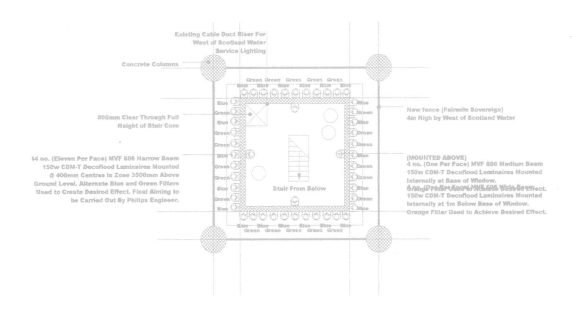

The effect was realised using a total of 44 narrow-beam 150W Decoflood CDM-T spotlights mounted around the base of the tower. The luminaires are housed inside a cage at the base of the stair core to protect them from theft and vandalism. The glazed stair core itself is lit from within using wide- and medium-beam 150W Decoflood CDM-T fixtures fitted with red and orange filters.

Prominent fins mounted externally around the perimeter of the main tank are downlit on each side with narrow blue beams, created by 24 Philips 70W Decoflood CDM-T spotlights. And the final touch is provided by four 55W low-pressure sodium fittings inside the glazed lantern on top of the tank, whose orange light contrasts with the blue and green hues below. The result is a striking 'beacon' for further regeneration of a socially disadvantaged area.

TEMPORARY AND NARRATIVE LIGHTING SCHEMES

In recent years, with the advent of more portable and durable theatre-style lighting equipment, we have seen the growth of temporary and narrative lighting projects, for commercial, promotional and artistic purposes. Such projects, often using colour, movement and image projection, usually permit a more dynamic and spectacular approach to lighting design than would be permitted for something more permanent. There are two broad approaches to such schemes, both of which are illustrated here – either the dramatic, all-action approach derived from French *son et lumière* or a more enigmatic, cerebral technique which shades off into the realms of lighting as art.

Tate Modern Gallery, London, UK

 St Paul's Cathedral, London, UK

 The Colosseum, Rome, Italy

 Sydney Opera House, Australia

 Flood, Meiho, Japan and Manningham Mill, Bradford, UK

COLOURFUL OPENING

Tate Modern Gallery
London, UK

The Tate Modern Gallery, on the south bank of the river Thames, is London's latest cultural attraction, housing the Tate Gallery's 20th-century collection of artworks and mounting a regular special programme of exhibitions. Costing around £134 million (much of it donated by the National Lottery), the gallery was created by Swiss architects Herzog & de Meuron by a clever and ambitious conversion of the derelict Bankside Power Station, designed by Sir George Gilbert Scott in 1947.

Herzog & de Meuron's conversion opens up the huge volume (155 by 35 by 23 metres) of the old turbine hall at the rear of the building as a one-off, toplit exhibition space, while seven new floors, including four floors of smaller galleries, have been inserted along the river façade. The former chimney in the centre of the building remains, topped by an internally illuminated light box, designed by artist Michael

Craig-Martin. Consequently the building retains its symmetrical, crucifix-shaped front elevation, facing the river and the new footbridge linking Bankside with St Paul's Cathedral in the City of London.

The new gallery was opened to huge public and media acclaim in May 2000 – and a major feature of the opening night was a spectacular *son et lumière* show, designed by exhibition design specialists, Imagination. The brief for the design of the temporary one-night lighting scheme 'was to keep it simple but surprising,' says Imagination's project lighting designer, Kate Wilkins. The project involved mainly theatrical-style fittings, which exploited the cross-like form of the elevation and relied on painting the vertical chimney block with **moving, shifting light.** This was combined with changing coloured lighting emanating from the horizontal glazing along the roofline.

These three photographs show the special treatment given to the central chimney, with projected colours
and beams of light overlaid with moving, open white lines (above and right).

The main luminaire for the chimney and front façade lighting was the VariLite VL5Arc fitting, which
provided a constant series of cross-fades and colour shifts. 'In order to cover the whole surface, the fittings
were located at two different offset positions,' explains Kate Wilkins. 'Half are mounted 15 metres from the
wall and the rest at about 30 metres.'

Superimposed onto this colour-flow effect were 10 Juliat d'Artagnan 2.5kW profile spotlights with
shutters. These projected moving open white lines up and down the chimney in a carefully choreographed
pattern. Laser technology also played its part in the spectacle. Six 30–50W laser projectors located across
the river were choreographed to throw a 4-minute repeating sequence of oblong and single-line laser
images across the building's exterior face.

The new, two-storey glazed roofline feature, known as the 'light beam', was also given a dual lighting
treatment. A total of 20 City Colors washlights by Studio Due with dichroic filters were set 4 metres out
from the glass, and put a **constant wash of colour** onto the gallery. At the same time a series of ETC
Source 4 luminaires, with gobo rotators, overlaid a moving texture effect along the roof. By creating this
moving texture effect, Imagination aimed to imitate the water reflections of the Thames in front of the Tate.

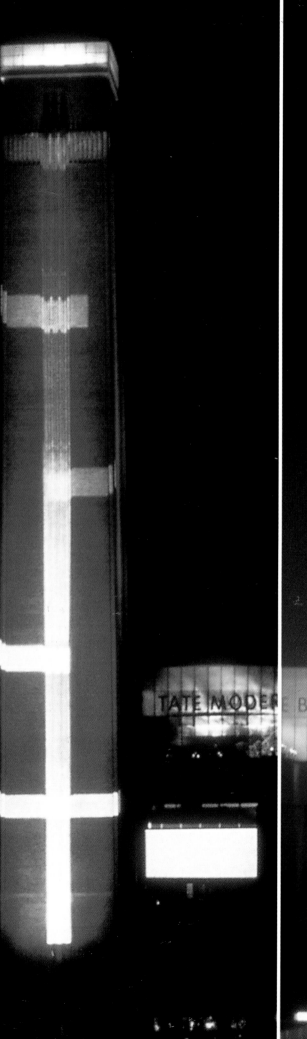

SCARLET CATHEDRAL

St Paul's Cathedral

London, UK

For temporary, 'one-off' events, lighting designers can often get away with effects that would be unacceptable on a permanent basis. One such project was a dramatic single-night lighting scheme for St Paul's Cathedral, Christopher Wren's baroque masterpiece in London. The scheme was designed by lighting designers Sutton Vane Associates (SVA) as a publicity event for Aids Awareness Day in late 1999. Commissioned by the London East Aids Network, the installation literally turned the front façade and dome of this world-famous building blood red.

The new lighting treatment contrasted starkly with St Paul's Cathedral's conventional floodlighting scheme, a pale and ghostly overall wash of white light, which was switched off for the evening. Using portable lighting equipment, installed by theatrical lighting specialists, Midnight Design, SVA set out to model the building's main details more effectively than the existing permanent scheme. 'We chose tungsten-halogen sources with red filters, because they permit easy dimming and fading, so different lighting elements could

be quickly balanced against each other on location,' explains SVA principal, Mark Sutton-Vane. 'And tungsten halogen contains so much red in its spectrum that filtering is relatively efficient.'

Every column on both porticos on the west façade, plus half the columns around the drum of the dome, was individually lit by narrow-beam spotlights. The dome itself was washed using wide-beam units, and the lantern picked out by narrow-beam spotlights. 'We wanted a degree of contrast, so we used **white light** from ultra-narrow-beam projectors to pick out the golden cross on the dome and the golden pineapples on the two west towers,' Sutton-Vane explains. 'This made them stand out wonderfully against the **red** of the rest of the building.'

The final *coup de grâce* was the dramatic build-up of the switch-on ceremony, to the sound of a slowly beating drum. First the lower portico faded up to full scarlet, followed by the upper portico, the two towers and the dome – the whole event seen later that evening on London TV news.

UNIQUE BEACON

The Colosseum
Rome, Italy

A scheme to illuminate Rome's famous Colosseum has taken the concept of lighting as narrative to a new and rather sombre dimension. Effectively, the ancient landmark was turned into a unique beacon against the death penalty for the Millennium year of 2000.

The high-profile campaign against capital punishment was backed by the Pope, Amnesty International, the United Nations and the Italian Government. Throughout the 12 months of the temporary installation, the ancient landmark had a window lit with white light for 48 hours following the news that a convict had been spared execution, or that a country had abandoned the death penalty. It was the perfect marriage of message, medium and means.

Clearly, the building is the perfect choice as a vehicle for the promotion: the Colosseum was chosen due to its historical links with death. Most famous are the defeated gladiators who had to plead with spectators in an attempt to be given a reprieve.It was built in 72AD by the Emperor Trajan, who once held games which lasted 117 days and included some 9,000 gladiators fighting to the death. Up to 50,000 spectators could be accommodated.

Lighting was the perfect medium to get a message across. As a non-intrusive medium, it is perfect for a national treasure whose integrity must be of paramount concern. There is also a transcendental, ethereal nature to light that speaks to something deep in our psyche, and it has symbolised life, hope and liberty for many centuries.

The campaign, termed The Colosseum Brightens Life Up, ran throughout the year and caught the mood of growing opposition to capital punishment in Italy. The organisers used the project as an example to garner support from the EU for an international effort against execution as punishment.

The 90kW lighting installation was designed and fitted by Rome's electricity utility ACEA, and included over 40 narrow-beam luminaires fitted with 2kW metal-halide lamps incorporating **golden-white** filters. The individual window lighting to mark the campaign's successes was augmented by the interior lighting, first used in 1999 to celebrate the anniversary of the start of the campaign. This was upgraded by ACEA with a 70W high-pressure sodium source to provide an effect as though the Sun is located within the central area of the rotunda.

The external scheme comprised a replacement of the previous installation and used 333 projector-style luminaires fitted with either 250W or 400W metal-halide lamps with a colour temperature of 3,200K.

'This is the first time a monument has been used for an inter-religious global campaign against the death penalty,' said Mario Marazziti of the Community of St Egidio, a Roman Catholic group which helped organise the launch ceremony. This included a specially made film with images of prisoners awaiting execution, protest demonstrations and data on capital punishment around the world.

The project was also a perfect example of how lighting, in the right context and with the right design, can be used effectively to tell a serious and thought-provoking story.

The Colosseum, chosen for its historical links with death, was turned into a unique beacon against the death penalty during the Millennium year of 2000, in a campaign backed by both the Pope and Amnesty International (left). A high-pressure sodium source located in the interior of the building creates an impression of the Sun shining out from the central rotunda (overleaf).

Se vuoi fermare la pena di morte, il 12 dicembre, fermati qui

AUTOMATIC PILOT

Sydney Opera House

Australia

Of all the world's great buildings, the Sydney Opera House has been used more than most for temporary lighting projections. This is no wonder, as Jorn Utzon's stunning design is a perfect canvas for projections — and reflections in the harbour water offer an added bonus.

Al Stone is the lucky lighting designer who has worked on all the major temporary schemes for the Opera House since 1998, including an installation for the Olympics in 2000. Perhaps the most ground-breaking of these projects, however, was his work for the annual Sydney Festival in January of the same year. This broke the previous pattern of temporary floodlight installations, introducing automated luminaires to explore some sophisticated design themes.

Stone teamed up with industrial designer, Marc Newson, for the conceptual design, and between them they developed a series of astronomical and psychedelic portraits that were turned into 180 full-colour custom gobos. But this was the easy bit. Projecting an even, crisp and well-illuminated image onto the complex sail-like roof of the Opera House from a limited number of available lighting positions was no simple matter.

For instance, on the east side of the building there is only one rigging position, the Man o' War jetty, but even this relies on considerable 'throw' distances of between 55 and 173 metres. Stone did a series of test illuminations during the summer of 1999 and concluded that no automated projector then manufactured had the high intensity required from these distant fitting locations.

Clearly, a custom-made fitting was needed. Stone approached Coemar De Sisti Australia, whose NAT
range had impressed him, and together with Coemar's senior design engineer in Italy, Fausto Orsati, they
developed the 4kW NAT MM 4000 with a zoom lens. 15 of these were used in the final installation,
along with two narrower-angle versions and nine 2.5kW units with rotation mirror heads. The moving
head units were from Coemar's 12kW CF range. For general wide-area floodlighting Stone specified
10 DMX-controlled Panorama units, also from Coemar. These fittings feature full, controllable
cyan-magenta-yellow colour mixing.

Perhaps Stone's most complicated task was to develop a masking gobo to fit the precise contours of the
building so that, when inserted in the rear gobo wheel of the NATs, it would provide accurate masking and
eliminate light spill beyond the building. He achieved this with the help of a specialist computer-rendering
agency, which modelled the Opera House digitally – and, using highly accurate information about the optics
and specification of the luminaires, he visualised the effects of the projections.

'On the first night, it was like putting together a giant jigsaw puzzle,' recalls programmer Megan McGahan.
'We had to rotate the gobos and adjust the heads until the design finally fell into place. I then programmed
a lot of alternative "looks" for both Al Stone and Marc Newson, until some final ideas were settled on.' The
result was a stunning 75-minute sequence that didn't rely on any moving beams. The team was then rightly
retained for the prestigious Olympics light show eight months later.

LIGHTING AS ART

Flood

Meiho, Japan

The medium of artificial light is increasingly used by artists to create spectacular, and often intriguing, temporary exterior installations – the high cost and lack of availability of suitable, exterior-rated lighting equipment being the main constraint on their greater permanence. However, there are now a growing number of well-known lighting artists working around the world, such as James Turrell, Dan Flavin, Peter Fink and Martin Richman (see pages 120–123). While full consideration of the broad range of lighting art lies outside the scope of this book, we would like to instantiate the trend by looking at two temporary installations by lighting artist Jim Buckley.

Manningham Mill

Bradford, UK

View of the 'Flood' installation, showing the five fish tanks brightly lit from within with different coloured lamps (left), and Manningham Mill, with the coloured projections shining out of the windows (right).

Back in 1993, Buckley used his work to help reclaim and restore an abandoned fish farm in Japan, using a colourful lighting installation, called appropriately, 'Flood'. He took five of the old fish tanks, each 2.5 by 7 by 1 metre in size, which were cleaned and their interiors painted white. 'The cultural significance of the fish pervades Japanese life, and this seemed a natural vehicle through which to realise the work,' Jim Buckley explains.

Within the tanks, which are full of flowing water, Buckley installed a number of **coloured underwater luminaires**, triggered by a photocell switch that operates the lighting at dawn and dusk. The light was constantly diffused and agitated by the water above, so they each appeared as mysterious pools of colour in the darkness – the project being very visible from a traffic and pedestrian bridge spanning a nearby gorge and river. The original project was intended to be temporary but it made such an impact that it became semi-permanent. And since the mid-1990s, the fish farm has been fully restored to its original use.

The animation of a derelict site was also a major feature of a later project, 'Fold' (1998), which took as its site an abandoned woollen mill in Bradford, UK, called Manningham Mill. 'The aim of the project was to draw attention to the building, using digital technology,' Buckley explains. 'I was keen to develop the obvious links with computers and the textile industry, particularly the use of punched cards to control Jacquard looms in weaving – similar cards were used in computing in the 1940s and '50s.'

In fact the installation, which was commissioned as part of the Photo '98 festival, involved digitising, colouring and animating a series of images of the woollen industry, derived from archive photos and video – and projecting them onto screens over 45 windows of the mill. From the outside, this ambitious projector installation, involving five computers and 15 projectors, 'created the impression of an enormous Jacquard loom weaving light inside the building.'

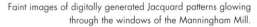

Faint images of digitally generated Jacquard patterns glowing through the windows of the Manningham Mill.

Close-up of the underwater lighting at Meiho – the effect constantly changed, due to the agitation of the water tanks.

GLOSSARY

Accent Lighting
Often used as a synonym for spotlighting; a technique of creating more intense areas of illumination on objects or surfaces.

Backlighting
A technique of lighting an object so that it is located between the viewer and the source, with the result that it is seen in relief or in silhouette.

Baffle
Device, often adjustable, attached to the front of a luminaire to limit light spill – often used synonymously with louvre.

Ballast
Electronic device which ignites the lamp and regulates the current through it.

Beam Angle
The measurement of the width of a light beam. The angle is defined in terms of the outer limits of the beam, where the light intensity declines to 50 per cent of maximum.

Busbar
Constant voltage circuit for connecting electrical equipment in parallel.

Cold Cathode
Often erroneously referred to as neon, this is a custom-made, low-pressure discharge lamp, usually in elongated lines or shapes, which can be made to emit highly saturated colour, using different gas additives. Most versions require a high voltage supply (over 1,000V), so public safety is a strong consideration in its use.

Colour Appearance
The apparent colour of light emitted by a particular light source – often expressed in terms of 'cool' and 'warm'.

Colour Rendering
The ability of a light source to give the colours of objects the same appearance as under a reference light source – usually daylight.

Colour Temperature
An objective measurement of the colour appearance of a lamp, measured in degrees Kelvin. The most commonly used lamps range from 2,700K ('warm') through 4,000K ('cool') to 6,000K ('cold').

Contrast
Subjective experience of comparative brightness between points or areas of luminance seen simultaneously, or successively. Too high a contrast difference can lead to glare.

Dichroic
A highly sophisticated form of glass, extensively used in reflectors and filters, which has the property of selectively filtering or reflecting different wavelengths of light, depending on the angle of incidence of the light beam.

Diffuse Lighting
Lighting which emanates evenly in all directions, with no predominant direction.

Direct Lighting
Lighting where most of the light from the luminaires reaches the surface directly, rather than being reflected from other surfaces.

Discharge Lamp
Large class of lamps, covering mercury vapour, sodium and metal halide, extensively used in commercial lighting. They work by using a high-voltage arc within the tube to ionise a mix of gases, which then glow powerfully.

Efficacy
The measured effectiveness of a lighting installation in converting electrical power to light, usually measured in lumens per watt (lm/W).

Fibre Optics
A light delivery system involving a remote conventional light source and series of light-transmitting glass or polymer cables. Light is projected down the fibre-optic 'tails' or cables, allowing the illumination of objects in sensitive or difficult locations or where a conventional luminaire would be too large.

Floodlighting
Often used erroneously to refer to all types of exterior lighting. More precisely, the often-abused technique of using wide-beam luminaires to illuminate large vertical or horizontal surfaces in a very uniform way.

Fluorescent Lamp
Fluorescent lamps are low-pressure discharge lamps, usually in a tubular or folded tube shape, in which the gas discharge produces (invisible) ultraviolet light, which in turn excites the phosphors coating the inside of the glass tube. These phosphors actually create the light.

Glare
The discomfort or impairment of vision experienced when parts of the visual field are excessively bright in relation to the general surroundings.

Gobo
A patterned screen device, usually made from glass or metal, and either stationary or rotating, located in the light beam of a projector or spotlight, to throw patterns or other simple images onto distant surfaces.

High-Pressure Sodium
Often referred to as HPS or SON, these discharge lamps rely on minute quantities of sodium within the discharge tube. Notable for their golden-yellow tint, they have fairly poor colour rendering and tend to flatten architectural details when used exclusively. The so-called 'white SON' lamp is a newer version that offers a whiter light, with better colour rendering – but low efficacy.

IALD
The International Association of Lighting Designers is the oldest and largest international organisation for independent lighting design consultants. It has an annual lighting design awards scheme for completed projects from around the world.

Incandescent lamp
The oldest type of commercially available lamp, in which light is produced by passing an electric current through a tungsten filament, so that it glows white hot. Very cheap to make with a fairly short life, the lamps are very inefficient, in that 90 per cent of their energy is emitted as heat, rather than light.

Indirect Lighting
Lighting in which the greater part of the light reaches the surface only after reflection from other surfaces.

Induction Lamp
A modern light source which has no filament or cathodes – a small electro-magnetic coil is used to create ultra-high-frequency waves that in turn vaporise mercury inside the lamp. The resulting ultra-violet then causes the phosphorescent coating on the glass to glow. Very long life and highly suitable for hard-to-access locations.

Lamp
The professional term for any artificial light source, colloquially known as a 'light bulb' – as distinct from the control apparatus surrounding the lamp (the luminaire).

Lamp Life
Manufacturers' stated operational life, at which (usually) 50 per cent of lamps are expected to fail under test conditions. Different manufacturers use different test conditions, so claims may vary for the same type and wattage of lamp.

LED
Light-emitting diode – the latest generation of lamps.

Light Pollution
Term designating the wasteful and unwanted spillage of light upwards above the horizontal, which can contribute to 'sky glow'.

Louvre
A screening device of vertical or horizontal (or both) blades, usually of aluminium or plastic, which cuts off the light beam at certain angles and prevents unwanted light spill.

Luminaire
Technical term for a light fitting – the apparatus that controls the distribution of light from the lamp source. It includes all the components necessary for fixing and protecting the lamps and for connecting them to the supply circuit.

Mercury Vapour
One of the first types of discharge lamp, producing a blue-white light, with rather poor colour rendering and only average energy efficiency.

Metal Halide
A discharge lamp that uses a mix of rare metal halides added to the discharge gas to create 'white' light. Have good colour rendering and fairly long life, particularly the new generation with ceramic, rather than quartz burners. These are often called CMH.

PAR Lamps
Short for parabolic aluminised reflector lamp, the PAR lamp has a sealed beam with its own integral aluminised reflector sprayed onto the rear surface of the lamp glass. PAR lamps therefore come in different fixed-beam angles and are usually either tungsten halogen or increasingly, metal halide. The number designation (PAR56, PAR38 etc.) refers to the size of the front face of the lamp in one-eighths of an inch (i.e. PAR38 is 4.75 inches wide).

Projector
Also known as profile spot. A theatrical-style spotlight, often with variable-focus optics, offering a range of beam distributions. It can usually be fitted with a number of accessories, such as gobos, filters, masks and so on, to enable accurate control over the shape and focus of the beam.

Reflectance
A measure of how effectively a surface will reflect light back, expressed as the ratio of light (lumens) falling on it and the light reflected off it (e.g. a reflectance of 0.8 is high, while 0.2 is low).

Searchlight
Very precise, powerful, narrow-beam spotlight derived from military use.

Scene Setting
The technique of using a computerised control system to offer a range of different lighting set-ups or conditions (scenes) to suit different times of day, uses and so on.

Source
Alternative word for lamp or light bulb.

Spill Light
Stray light from a luminaire that incidentally illuminates nearby objects or surfaces – in the public environment, this can be a major cause of 'light trespass'.

Spreader Lens
A special lens made from ribbed glass that can elongate a symmetrically shaped beam either vertically or horizontally, to precisely illuminate a tall or wide object.

Strobe
A high-intensity flashing white light used for surprise or decorative effect.

Tungsten Halogen
A refinement on the older type of incandescent tungsten lamp, in which a small amount of halogen within the glass envelope helps to recycle tungsten vapour back to the filament, to prolong its life.

Uniformity
The ratio of the minimum illuminance to the maximum illuminance over a specified surface.

Uplighter
Broad term to describe a luminaire that either bounces most of its light off the ceiling or other matt surface – or any fitting that is used to light a building or object from below.

Xenon Lamp
An arc discharge lamp containing pure xenon, characterised by a spectral output of around 6,500K – similar to daylight. As the lamps pack a lot of power into a small source, they are used in cinema projectors and searchlights.

USEFUL ADDRESSES

International Association of Lighting Designers (IALD), Merchandise Mart, Suite 487, 200 World Trade Center, Chicago, Illinois 60654, USA
Tel: +1 312 527 3677 Fax: +1 312 527 3680
www.iald.org

Institution of Lighting Engineers (ILE), Lennox House, 9 Lawford Road, Rugby CV21 2DZ, UK
Tel: +44 (0)1788 576 492 Fax: +44 (0)1788 540 145

Society of Light and Lighting c/o CIBSE, Delta House, 222 Balham High Road, London SW12 9BS, UK
Tel: +44 (0)20 8675 5211 Fax: +44 (0)20 8675 5449
www.cibse.org

English Heritage, Fortress House, PO Box 569, Swindon SN2 2YP, UK
Tel: +44 (0)1793 414 910 Fax: +44 (0)1793 414 926
www.english-heritage.org.uk

Royal Town Planning Institute (RTPI), 26 Portland Place, London W1N 4BE, UK
Tel: +44 (0)20 7636 9107 Fax: +44 (0)20 7323 1582
www.rtpi.org.uk

The Landscape Institute, 6 Barnard Mews, London SW11 1QU, UK
Tel: +44 (0)20 7738 9166 Fax: +44 (0)20 7350 5201
www.l-i.org.uk

Architecture Commission and the Built-in Environment, 7 St James's Square, London SW1Y 4JU, UK
Tel: +44 (0)20 7839 6537 Fax: +44 (0)20 7839 8475
www.cabe.org.uk

Lighting Industry Federation, 207 Balham High Road, London SW12 7BQ, UK
Tel: +44 (0)20 8675 5432 Fax: +44 (0)20 8673 5880
www.lif.co.uk

USEFUL PUBLICATIONS

Designing with Light – Public Spaces, Turner, J., 1998
Designing with Light – Retail Spaces, Turner, J., 1998
Designing with Light – Bars and Restaurants, Entwistle, J., 1999
Designing with Light – Hotels, Entwistle, J., 2000
All the above are published by RotoVision

Lighting Design: An Introductory Guide for Professionals, Gardner, C and Hannaford, B., Design Council, 1993
A–Z of Lighting Terms, Fitt, B., Heinemann, 1999
The Design of Lighting, Treganza, P and Loe, D., E&FN SON, 1998
Lighting, Niesewand, N., Mitchell & Beazley, 1999
Catching the Light, Jajonc, A., Bantam Books, 1995
Lighting the Environment: A Guide to Good Urban Lighting, CIBSE/ILE, 1995
Lighten our Darkness: Lighting our Cities – Successes, Failures and Opportunities, Royal Fine Art Commission, 1994
Lighting Historic Buildings, Phillips, D., Architectural Press, 1997
Lighting Modern Buildings, Phillips, D., Architectural Press, 2000

CREDITS

Introduction: p8–9 courtesy of Robin Scagell at Galaxy Picture Library (except p9, left, courtesy of Dúchas, The Heritage Service); p10 (top left and right) courtesy of Michael Hue-Williams at Fine Art Ltd., and p10 (bottom) courtesy of Metropolitan Museum of Art, New York, USA/Bridgeman Art Library; p11 courtesy of the Italian State Tourist Board, (E.N.I.T) London; p12 (top) courtesy of Victory Lighting, and p12 (bottom left and right) courtesy of LDP Ltd./Pinniger & Partners; p13 (top left and right) courtesy of LDP Ltd., and p13 (bottom) courtesy of iGuzzini; p14 (left) courtesy of IALD, and p14 (right) photograph by Brett; p15 courtesy of Kim Lighting. **New Buildings**: p18–21 courtesy of DHA and photographs by Richard Holttum at Light & Lighting magazine, ed. Brian Sims; p22–23 courtesy of Cline Bettridge Bernstein Lighting and photographs (left) courtesy of IALD and (right) by Timothy Hursley; p24–7 courtesy of PHA Lighting and photographs courtesy of IALD; p28–31 courtesy of Philips Lighting; p32–3 courtesy of Motoko Ishii Lighting Design/IALD and photographs by Yoichi Yamazaki; p34–7 courtesy of Speirs and Woodruffe/JSA; p38–41 courtesy of I.M.Pei/Fisher Marantz Renfro Stone and photographs by Timothy Hursley. **Heritage and Historic Buildings**: p44–9 courtesy of © S.N.T.E/Louis Poulsen; p50–1 courtesy of LDP Ltd.; p52–5 courtesy of Graham Phoenix at lightmatters/IALD; p56–61 courtesy of iGuzzini. **Squares and Public Spaces**: p64–7 courtesy of Esudio de Diseño NEDEA-MADRID/Philips Lighting; p68–73 courtesy of Gabriel Design and diagrams courtesy of Philips Lighting; p74–7 courtesy of Ross de Alessi Lighting Design and photographs courtesy of IALD; p78–81 courtesy of Speirs & Major/JSA; p82–5 courtesy of Equation Lighting Design/SD&P Architects and photographs © D.E.L Graphics; p86–7 courtesy of LDP Ltd. **Bridges and Towers**: p90–3 courtesy of Robert Daniels of Brilliant Lighting Design; p94–7 courtesy of Yann Kersale and photographs by Christophe Hascoér; p98–9 courtesy of JSA; p100–3 courtesy of Motoko Ishii Lighting Design and photographs by Yoichi Yamazaki; p104–7 courtesy of Focus Lighting; p108–13 courtesy of GE Lighting; p114–117 courtesy of Robert Daniels at Brilliant Lighting Design. **Industrial Plants and Structures**: p120–5 courtesy of Martin Richman and photographs by Anthony Oliver (except p122–3 and p125, bottom right, photographs by Martin Richman); p126–9 courtesy of Ross De Alessi Lighting Design and photographs courtesy of IALD; p130–3 courtesy of Jonathan Park/I.B.A. Meiderich Ltg and photographs by Lars Behrendt (except for p133 photograph by Jonathan Park); p134–7 courtesy of Chris Stewart Architects/Philips Lighting and photographs by Adrian Stewart. **Temporary and Narrative Lighting Schemes**: p140–3 courtesy of Imagination; p144–5 courtesy of SVA; p146–9 courtesy of Associated Press and photographs by Marco Ravagli; p150–151 courtesy of Al Stone/Marc Newson/Coemar de Sisti Australia; p152–5 courtesy of Jim Buckley and photographs by Jim Buckley (except p153 photograph by Jim Hamlyn © Guzzelian).

ACKNOWLEDGEMENTS

We would like to thank the following for their encouragement and assistance in collating material and photography for this book: Jill Entwistle, Bob Daniels, Martin Richman, Morag Fullilove, Phil Gabriel, Paul Gregory, James Hooker, Erik Holm of Louis Poulsen, the unbelievably helpful Matteo Negri of Associated Press, Barbara Wheeler and Franka Heesterbeek at Philips Lighting, Adrian Kitching at GE Lighting, Rowan Crowley at EMAP, and Jonathan Speirs, Mark Major and Julie and Shelley at the Lighting Architects Group. Our special thanks also go to Erica Ffrench at RotoVision for her support and organisation.

The Publisher would also like to thank Anna Heinrich, Leon Palmer and Peter Struycken for their invaluable help and advice at the beginning of the project, and RotoVision's Editor-in-Chief Natalia Price-Cabrera for devising the series concept.

INDEX

Akashi Kaikyo Bridge, Japan 100–3
Albert Memorial, London 52–5

Banco Colpatria Tower, Bogotá 90–3
Bideau, Pierre 45
brightness 13, 53
Brilliant Lighting Design 90, 115
Buckley, Jim 152–5
Burj Al Arab, Dubai 98–9

ceramic lamps 67, 77, 112
Chain Bridge, Budapest 108–13
Chris Stewart Architects 135
City of Bridges, Cleveland 126–9
Cline Bettridge Bernstein Lighting 22
cold cathode lamps 83, 132
Colosseum, Rome 146–9
colour 13, 51, 67, 84, 109, 144
    changes 33, 35, 80, 93,
    99, 103, 124
    filters 14, 37, 96, 116, 132
    temperature 27, 29, 60, 73,
    85, 147
computer-controlled lighting 14, 80,
104–7, 155
Cranhill Water Tower, Glasgow 134–7
Croydon Town Centre, UK 78–81

David Hersey Associates 19
dichroic filters 51, 105, 128, 142
dimming and fading 144
downlighting 91, 137
dynamic effects 14, 37

Efteling Fairground, Tilborg 28–31
Eiffel Tower, Paris 44–9
Enriques, Francisco Alcon 65
Entel Tower, Chile 104–7
Equation Lighting Design 83
Estuarine Habitats and Coastal
Fisheries Center, Louisiana 22–3

125, 132, 151
fluorescent lamps 21, 96, 112, 116,
132
Gabriel Design 69
gas lights 45, 87
gobos 142, 150–1

Downtown Helsinki, Finland 74–7
Hong Kong Convention Centre,
Hong Kong 24–7

iGuzzini 57
Imagination 79, 141
Imax Cinema, London 18–21
incandescent lamps 48
induction lamps 33, 101

Jonathan Speirs and Associates 99

Kersale, Yann 95

Landscheftspark, Duisberg-Nord
130–3
lasers 142
lenses 54, 132, 151
light-emitting diodes 37
LDP Ltd. 51, 53, 87
lighting poles 69, 77, 84
Lighting Technology Projects 130
luminaires 37, 51, 54, 77, 87, 99,
112, 137, 142, 147, 150

McArthur Causeway Bridge, Miami
114–17
Manningham Mill, Bradford 153, 155
metal halide lamps 27, 29, 37, 38,
77, 109, 115, 125, 128, 132, 147
Metso, Eero 75
Miho Museum, Shigaraki 38–41
Millennium Dome, London 34–7
mirrors 91–3
Motoki Ishii Lighting Design 33, 100
MR16 lights 23

Newson, Marc 150
Northern Lights 135

Peace Gardens, Sheffield 82–5
PHA Lighting 27
Philips Lighting 29, 65
photocells 21, 128, 155
Plaza de España, Valladolid 64–7
polycarbonate light pipes 125
Pont de Normandie, Le Havre 94–7
projectors 80, 83, 93, 96, 99, 124,
132, 142, 145, 150–1, 155

reflected light 73, 87
remote source lighting 53–4, 66
Richman, Martin 121
Ross De Alessi Lighting Design 75,
128

saturated colour 14, 79, 105, 131
searchlights 99, 107
Smithfield Public Space, Dublin 86–7
sodium lamps 29, 60, 96, 128, 137,
147
Speirs & Major 37, 80
spotlights 19, 21, 37, 51, 54, 87,
115, 137, 145
St Paul's Cathedral, London 144–5
Stone, Al 150
strobe flash units 80, 99
Sutton Vane Associates 144
Sydney Opera House, Australia 150–1

Tate Modern Gallery, London 140–3
Teflon fabric 34, 99
Temple of Luxor, Egypt 56–61
Trinity Buoy Wharf, London 50–1
tungsten halogen lamps 37, 60, 144
Tyseley Waste Plant, Birmingham
120–5

Unilever House, London 15
uplighters 21, 57, 77, 83, 87

VariLite 104–5

washlights 35, 142
water features 73, 84, 155
Woodruffe, Patrick 35